Telemarketer's Handbook

Telemarketer's Handbook

PROFESSIONAL TACTICS & STRATEGIES FOR INSTANT RESULTS

Darlene Maciuba-Koppel

AT&T Marketing Manager for Voice Products

 Sterling Publishing Co., Inc.   New York

Library of Congress Cataloging-in-Publication Data
Maciuba-Koppel, Darlene.
    Telemarketer's handbook : professional tactics & strategies for
instant results / by Darlene Maciuba-Koppel.
        p.   cm.
    Includes bibliographical references and index.
    ISBN 0-8069-8242-X
    1. Telemarketing—Handbooks, manuals, etc.   I. Title.
HF5415.1265.M32   1992
658.8'4—dc20   91-42682
                                                                    CIP

10   9   8   7   6   5   4   3   2   1

Published in 1992 by Sterling Publishing Company, Inc.
387 Park Avenue South, New York, N.Y. 10016
Copyright © 1992 AT&T
Distributed in Canada by Sterling Publishing
% Canadian Manda Group, P.O. Box 920, Station U
Toronto, Ontario, Canada M8Z 5P9
Distributed in Great Britain and Europe by Cassell PLC
Villiers House, 41/47 Strand, London WC2N 5JE, England
Distributed in Australia by Capricorn Link Ltd.
P.O. Box 665, Lane Cove, NSW 2066
Manufactured in the United States of America
All rights reserved

Sterling ISBN 0-8069-8242-X Paper

Acknowledgments

I'd like to thank the following for their contributions: N. Powell Taylor, general manager of the GE Answer Center; Richard L. Bencin, president of Richard L. Bencin & Associates; Steve Riddell, telemarketing center manager of Blue Cross/ Blue Shield of Virginia; Robert Clark, AT&T vice president; Thomas Rotkowski, center manager of Day-Timers, Inc.; and my husband, Ronald Koppel, AT&T telemarketing marketing manager, for his support.

CONTENTS

Telemarketer's Handbook

INTRODUCTION

Telemarketing is your ticket to marketing success. Although this discipline has been around for many years, recent advances in telecommunications technology greatly enhance telemarketing as a significant cost-effective marketing tool.

Telemarketing is also able to touch your customers in a very immediate, emotional, and personal way. Through telemarketing, you can generate, identify, and track potentially profitable prospects.

Telemarketing is responsive to change. This characteristic enables the telemarketing manager to be innovative and to step in either when a campaign needs adjustment or to increase sales. Telemarketing is also conducive to testing and pilot programs.

This book aims to provide helpful hints, resources to use for "right now" ideas, teaching tips, problem-solvers, and inspiration. The book will help you keep going, obtain quick knowledge, and save you some learning time.

My background at AT&T includes telemarketing sales and management, advertising, promotion, customer service, and product marketing. Telemarketing presents the most exciting challenge to me. The discipline may be hectic and frustrating, but telemarketing offers many opportunities for creativity. I regard a telemarketing center as a "learning lab" for managers—a place to test new ideas, to stretch the imagination, to experiment, to take a quick risk, to develop new procedures, and to help people grow.

Use this book as a reference tool for quick access to information when you face a particular challenge, or use it as an idea source. I know time is tight, so don't read this book cover-to-cover. Instead, read it in bite-size chunks during those spare moments when you need inspiration or just some quick facts.

The first chapter, "Telemarketing Plan," describes how to get started, how to manage a pilot program, and it offers a telemarketing checklist. Read about recruiting successful reps in chapter two. The uses of role-play are discussed there, as well as the importance of ongoing training.

"Monitoring" explains the benefits that this practice brings to your reps and to your company. How to build a good monitoring program is also described. Script-writing is explained in chapter four. Every step is covered, from opening the call, to closing the sale, and to the value of objections.

Avoid telemarketing failures by reading chapter five. The importance of monitoring all aspects of your center and your data bases, and the mistakes you don't want to make are all covered. This chapter also tells why it's good to look for trouble in your center. As a manager, it's up to you to create a motivational environment there. In chapter six, you'll find that there's more than one way to motivate.

Chapter seven, "Tracking," shows that what you measure is what you get, and describes the benefits of tracking. What do you do when things aren't working?

Turn to chapter eight. This chapter lists some tough questions to ask yourself. Perhaps you'll uncover solutions for your center.

This is the age of customer service, and chapter nine shows what you should be doing to create a customer-focused center, and how important it is to fix the inside first. You will read about complaints and the opportunities they present, and how to improve customer satisfaction. In chapter ten, you'll read about *Integrated Direct Marketing* (IDM), a methodology that will help you enhance both your telemarketing contacts and your profits. Use these ideas as your key to telemarketing success.

1
TELEMARKETING PLAN

Telemarketing is a powerful tool; it can exert a positive and profitable impact on your company. You won't find telemarketing in some neat package ready to be picked from the shelf. No two companies, programs, or campaigns are alike. A telemarketing program has to be designed to fit a particular organization, with its unique objectives and specific requirements. This undertaking isn't simple. Telemarketing requires careful planning, well-thought-out structuring, and continual measuring and testing.

If you're new to telemarketing, your first step may be to sell the concept to management. Then, move on to reviewing your company's current marketing operations, and determining how telemarketing will fit in. If you manage a telemarketing center, each new campaign offers you the opportunity to review the basics of telemarketing, and to pick up new tips that can add to your success. An experienced center manager has the advantage of using the knowledge gained from previous campaigns to plan new promotions. Careful analysis of past promotions can prevent the repetition of the same mistakes, and it fosters innovation by taking a routine task and adding a twist.

As a telemarketing center manager, you must relearn, review, and redo the basics as presented in the following chapter, and further detailed in some of the subsequent chapters. Once you master these basics, it's time to take bits of telemarketing knowledge from here and there, and continually integrate, experiment, and test, aiming to be more successful each time.

Where Does Telemarketing Fit In?

Telemarketing can't operate in a vacuum, or only be used as a "quick fix" when sales are down. Telephone sales comprise only one part of the whole process. To make telemarketing work, it must be an integral part of your company's overall marketing efforts. A successful telemarketing program is ongoing, well planned, and an important part of your organization's marketing scheme.

If you want a winning telemarketing program, get all levels of management to support the process. This includes informing and working with the field-sales force, thereby warding off any potential resentment. Show the field-sales force how telemarketing can complement its sales efforts, and show how it won't compete against it. This will promote team spirit, and success. Telemarketing should be recognized as a powerful tool in the sales environment—as important as the outside sales force, direct mail, and promotional campaigns.

Powell Taylor, manager of the GE Answer Center, says,

> Most of the problems I see in telemarketing are due to an inability to sell telemarketing to management. New-center execution sometimes lacks

commitment to resources and professionalism. Management skimps on pay and training, and the *best* sales people aren't used for business-to-business.

Build an Outbound Telemarketing Process

Identify the market

Begin the telemarketing process by carefully targeting your market. Who is your market? Your best prospects for additional sales are usually your current and past customers. Lists are another source of prospects.

Obtain response lists. These lists contain names of people who have recently responded to direct media such as direct mail and TV commercials. These people are usually receptive to purchasing from your company. Generate these lists from in-house promotional programs. Rent or purchase customer lists from companies similar to your own.

Buy "compiled" lists. Prospects who meet a set of common criteria make up these lists.

Which list to use? Base your decision on your knowledge of the market. Which list best meets your typical customer profile?

Since the quality of the lists used will directly affect the success or failure of your telemarketing program, it doesn't pay to save a few dollars on a list.

Define the offer

A complete offer includes: the product or service, price, and the delivery system. Delivery includes the process of getting the product to the customer, and the receipt of payment by the seller.

Kinks can often develop in the delivery system. During one company's campaign, the telemarketing center neglected to send computer tapes containing the customer orders to the fulfillment house. Meanwhile, the fulfillment vendor didn't know that the campaign had indeed started, and didn't think that anything was wrong. A good system of quality checks could have avoided this mishap, which resulted in delayed delivery to the customers.

Choose a medium

Examine your existing sales processes and decide how they'll best support your telemarketing program. Combine the two efforts to achieve a synergy that a stand-alone telemarketing campaign can't provide.

The telephone's one drawback is that it's a one-dimensional medium. It lacks the "punch" provided by the colorful illustrations of print or direct-mail offers. The expressive body language of the salesperson in action and the concrete credibility of print are also missing. Take advantage of the power of television, radio, direct mail, print advertising, and your field-sales force to multiply your sales advantage. Be aware of some of the limitations of the different media. Radio and television don't do as well as other media when complex messages need to be presented.

Refine the message

Your product and service will determine the type of script you'll use.

Verbatim script These scripts are generally used in business-to-consumer calls. Telephone sales representatives (TSRs) follow the scripts word for word, and the message is usually brief. Calls can range from three to four minutes. The script contains 350–500 words, depending upon the complexity of the product being sold. Although the scripts are followed word-for-word, proper coaching can prevent the script from sounding "canned."

Guided script A guided script is less restrictive than a verbatim script. It allows the rep to adjust the direction of the presentation according to the progress of his conversation with the customer. This format usually works best in business-to-business calls, but it can be used in business-to-consumer calls when the product offered requires the rep to do some probing. The script can contain two or three open- and closed-ended probing questions. Script length averages about 500–750 words, and it can take from five to six minutes to deliver.

Outline script The TSR has near-total flexibility with this format. The script contains words and ideas written in outline form. A probing sequence is used with this type of presentation. The call can last about seven minutes, but it should never run longer than ten minutes, except when the rep and the customer have a strong relationship.

The information offered above consists of general suggestions. The script that's best for your telemarketing center is the script that will give you the best results. The only way to determine a script's usefulness is to continually test and revise it. You may find that a verbatim script works for one campaign, while another campaign requires an outline script.

Set up a strategic plan

A strategic plan ensures that all levels of management have carefully thought about the company's goals. The plan also provides future guidance for employees. It details what your telemarketing department proposes to do, how it proposes to carry out the plan, and how much the program will cost. The plan should include department objectives, strategies, step-by-step implementation, and list the needed resources and funds. Specific strategies need to be developed to determine how you'll reach each client segment. Your strategic plan must also describe your strategy for serving your customers.

Questions to Ask Yourself

When you begin planning, ask yourself the following questions: "Who are my customers?" "What are their ages?" "What are their income levels?"

Maintain an accurate customer data base or a clear customer profile. Your customer profile is constantly changing. You must continually research your customer market and update your data base. Use this research to win more business customers by locating additional contacts within a company to which you're currently marketing. Take a second look at your current customer profile, using it as a guide for finding new prospects in the marketplace.

Where are your customers? The answer to this question helps you determine which geographic area to target.

What is the objective of your campaign? Is it to sell a product/service, or to generate leads? What must you do to achieve your objective?

What is your product or service? Define your company in terms of your product or service to create a successful strategic plan.

What are your customers' expectations? Determine their expectations by telephone surveys, by mailing questionnaires, or by holding focus groups. You can only build a customer-satisfaction plan if you know what satisfies your customers. You can then meet customer expectations by anticipating their needs and meeting them. Establish your company as best-in-class and superior to the competition. Last, when will your campaign begin?

Create a Consumer–Customer Profile

Use the following attributes to help you create a profile of a typical consumer customer: age, sex, address, phone number, credit history, marital status, number of children, income, life-style, interests, and use of similar products and services.

Create a Business–Customer Profile

To create a business-customer profile, determine these characteristics: company name, address, phone number, business size (revenue, locations, number of employees); decision maker/main contact name and title, Standard Industrial Classification (SIC) code, and products/services manufactured/sold. Also determine whom the company sells to, how many years it's been in business, if the company uses products/services similar to your own, the company's credit history, its goals and objectives, its plans for expansion, its competitors, and its average cost per sale.

Sell Telemarketing to Your Company

You believe that telemarketing would be a lucrative addition to your company's current marketing plan. How do you sell the idea to top management? Become a "salesperson" for telemarketing. For any sales or marketing technique to work, the people who implement the new technique must be thoroughly convinced that it's the right approach. As a good "salesperson," first understand to whom you're selling and adjust your strategy accordingly. Analyze your company's style and attitudes to help you determine how to "sell" telemarketing, and whether to implement the telemarketing pilot program in-house or off-site.

To get things done, managers must develop informal power. First, they must accept the organization as it is, learn how it works, and how to manipulate it. In any formal organization, there's an informal organization. Understandings are reached, causes are advanced, and alliances are formed in private meetings. It's always safer to first work things out unofficially before going public. Managers need to determine risks, positions, attitudes, resources, and timing. This work is undocumented, and off the record. However, this is where things happen. Coming up with ideas without consulting others can result in failure, no matter how greatly researched, thoughtfully conceived and documented. Making formal presentations on new ideas without first informally consulting with others can result in ideas falling on deaf ears. Presenting a new idea at a meeting is also risky. If the idea doesn't get support, it may never get another chance. In private encounters, people can reach decisions informally; managers can test their proposals to make sure they'll work before going public. They can seek out allies, find common interests. Quiet work with a few friendly compatriots gives you a better understanding of what's acceptable in your company.

Use the "divide and conquer" method to promote the telemarketing program to upper-level management. Arrange one-on-one meetings where you can informally present your ideas. Take note of criticisms and suggestions and revise your presentation accordingly. Later, call the entire "presold" group together to make a formal presentation and sale.

Pilot Program

If your company is new to the field, the best way to test telemarketing is to set up a pilot program. In fact, it's also a good idea to pilot any new campaigns before they begin. What's a pilot? A telemarketing pilot is a small-scale program established to handle one specific marketing or sales activity for a set period of time.

The benefits of a pilot program are many. A pilot provides you with measurable results to determine the profitability of telemarketing. It also allows you to see firsthand how telemarketing works, determines response patterns to questions, anticipates customers' objections, and identifies any problems. Pilots provide quick feedback on your overall program. By using the same script employed in the pilot, sales probability can be determined for the actual campaign. You can also determine campaign objectives, get the kinks out, polish up the scripts, allow for retraining of reps (if necessary), and the opportunity to evaluate your lists of prospects.

A pilot program should include a limited market area that exhibits the same traits as your total target market. The customer base of a pilot program is usually small. Test a pilot on your regular customers first, before you attempt the program on untested groups or lists.

The number of personnel (reps, supervisors) in a pilot is limited. Pilots should only last long enough to provide measurable results. The pilot period should be short enough so that it won't interfere with full implementation of your telemarketing program. An ideal pilot program for a new start-up is from three to six months long. A new campaign pilot, in an established center, usually runs from two to three weeks.

Track the following data in a pilot program: number of contacts made daily, weekly, and monthly, the number of contact attempts, the number of sales, and the number of contacts per sale. Other data tracked include: sales expenses (salary, commission of reps), communication costs (monthly costs of 800 numbers, WATS lines, etc.), net profit, average call length, length of contact, length of sales call, and conversion rate (the rate of sales to completed contacts). Management Information Systems ("MIS," systems that supply sales-support information which the specialist needs to perform a function) are crucial to implement and evaluate the pilot program's performance. The information needs to be timely, easily accessible, and accurate. For a pilot program, the system can be manual, computerized, or a combination of both. Take these steps to design your MIS:

- Define MIS needs with your telemarketing reps in mind.
- Determine what information is needed for smooth communication with other departments in your firm.
- Define management's specific information needs.
- Decide between a manual system or a computerized system to meet the needs above.
- Consider the cost, productivity, and efficiency for your program.

Carefully assess the results of your pilot program, so you can plan for a successful campaign. Pay attention to the following factors.

- Analyze the strengths of the pilot.
- List the weaknesses of the pilot.
- Look at your measurements.
- What has telemarketing told you about your business?
- Study the buying patterns of your customers.
- Evaluate the advertising you used during the pilot.
- Did some advertisements pull in more leads than others? Why?
- Examine the profitability measurements.
- If your objective was to increase overall sales, measure your total sales volume.
- Did your pilot meet original objectives? (By answering this question you can set realistic objectives for full implementation of your program.)
- Look at the profitability of your pilot. Compare the revenue to the expense of a telemarketing call.
- Improve the pilot program before full implementation.

Target Marketing

Follow the lead of the direct-mail experts. Use list segmentation and profiling techniques to target your market. For example, if you're selling a long-distance calling service, you may have prospects who are heavy users of long distance, medium users, or prospects who don't make any long-distance calls. Within these segments, you can identify even smaller segments: business travellers, college students, and military personnel, for example.

When targeting markets, balance the difficulty of the market to be penetrated with the cost of the telephone contact.

Timing

Your timing needs to be right if you're promoting seasonal items. Promote Christmas products in September. Any later than that, and you may miss the season.

Be sensitive to your customers' feelings. Don't call consumers on holidays, including certain ethnic or religious holidays. Don't call during the Super Bowl, or an election night.

You'll reach more customers if you call during the following hours. To reach consumers, call Monday through Friday 5 P.M.–9 P.M. local time. On Saturday call between 10 A.M.–9 P.M. local time. On Sunday call between 1:30 P.M.–9 P.M. local time. For business customers, call Monday through Friday 9 A.M.–6 P.M. local time.

With the residential market, you risk irritating the customer if you make calls after 9 P.M. The same goes for calling customers before 10 A.M. on Saturday. What about calling consumers during the day from Monday through Friday? Do some test calls and see if this works for your company. The advent of predictive dialling (The computer system dials a call, anticipating when the rep will be available to handle another call. The system then transfers only "live" calls to the rep.) can make calling during the day cost-effective.

With business customers, you'll have some luck reaching upper-level management by calling either very early in the morning, after business hours, or during lunch hour. These are the times when executives are likely to answer their phones themselves.

Business-to-Business vs. Business-to-Consumer Telemarketing

The objectives and requirements of business-to-business telemarketing and business-to-consumer telemarketing are very different. Keep these differences in mind when you set up your specific program. Manage business and residential campaigns separately. Some comparisons of these two disciplines follow.

Business-to-Business

Outbound
5 to 8 completed calls per hour
$6–$10 per call per decision-
maker contact

Inbound
$2.50–$5 per call

Training
Extensive training in technical or
specialized products or services

Business-to-Consumer

Outbound
10 to 15 completed calls per hour
$2.50–$4 per call per decision-
maker contact

Inbound
$1.50–$3 per call

Training
Emphasize speed of call
Emphasize getting an order

Inbound/Outbound Cost

The cost for various inbound/outbound telemarketing campaigns varies with the complexity of the campaigns. Consequently, it's prudent to calculate costs for each campaign.

Order processing, customer service, and sales promotion are low-cost, while sales support and account management are high-cost.

Outbound Rep vs. Inbound Rep

Outbound Rep
Needs to be aggressive
Must possess good selling skills
Requires three (or more) weeks'
training before he can work
alone and be productive

Inbound Rep
Needs extensive training on
products and services
Needs to answer questions
Solves problems
Handles complaints and general
customer service
Requires four (or more) weeks of
training

Sales Sequence—Outbound Business-to-Business Call

Business-to-business pre-call planning

Before you make your first call, you should know the customer's business and have thought through the call. You should be able to predict the prospect's objections, and be ready with convincing rebuttals. Know your own product information, know your customer and his company, know your personal objectives, and set specific call objectives. Last, prepare an opening statement, fact-finding questions, and a sales message.

Effective steps in a business telemarketing call

Use all of the steps, in order, with smooth transitions.

- Identify yourself and your firm.
- Establish rapport.
- Give the purpose of the call and create interest.
- Ask fact-finding questions.
- Deliver your sales message.
- Answer objections.
- Close the sale.
- Wrap up the call.

Business-to-business follow-up

Follow-up measures ensure that you've actually produced an order, both for your customer and for your own company. Until the order is delivered and paid for, it isn't complete.

Add-On Selling

Many centers use add-on selling to increase the value of a telephone sale. Since you already have the customer on the line, and the initial sale has already been made, the prospects for an add-on sale are likely. However, plot every step of the process before you begin. Here are some idea-starters.

- Make sure the reps are knowledgeable about both the products and the add-ons.
- Determine your strategy. Which products will you add on? What are the prices of the add-ons? Who is your target market? Is the campaign ongoing or short-term? How will you incorporate verbiage into your script to sell an add-on?
- Complete the initial sales order first, and then proceed to the add-on presentation.
- Choose add-on items that make enough profit to justify the cost of the additional time spent on the phone.
- Reps should only sell those add-ons that are related to the product or service the customer has just purchased.
- Don't sell add-ons to get rid of excess stock or discontinued items unless you inform your customers of your intention.
- Do a trial campaign first, with a limited number of add-on items.
- If the trial is successful, create an incentive program for your reps to increase the sale of add-ons.

- Promote only those items the customer is familiar with, thereby decreasing the amount of talk time required to sell the add-ons.
- The price of the add-on should be reasonable, no more than 20–30% of the overall cost of the order.

"Growing" an Application

Day-Timers, Inc., of Allentown, PA, is the world's largest producer of time-management tools, such as planners, diaries, and accessories. Tom Rotkowski, manager of the telemarketing center, says,

> We began our operation by hiring reps to be direct-entry personnel. They were trained to take phone calls, not sell. We have since evolved to training our people to be telesales agents. Using telesales techniques, they are able to do consultative selling, open probing, and overcoming objections.

Day-Timers is an example of how a company moved from efficiently processing orders to providing a value-added service to its customers.

During calls, reps are encouraged to: cross-sell, promote accessory items, and upgrade the customer's current products. Reps use a discussion process that includes product knowledge, probing, questions, and listening to what the customer is saying about the product, his needs, or his life-style. These questions enable the rep to develop a strategy to suggest the products that best match the customer.

Since "teleselling" adds thirty seconds to each call, it's an expensive proposition that takes careful planning, and successful implementation, with vigilant watchdogging all the way.

Formula for Success

Powell Taylor describes the GE Answer Center's formula for success.

People

Prospects must go through a rigorous selection process. Intensive training comes next. Once on the job, the reps are regularly motivated to keep them sharp. And, "training never stops," says Taylor.

Environment

Work stations are roomy, well organized, and private. The center is well lighted and bathed in soft tones of color.

Technology

Technology is tops at the telemarketing center. Reps have access to the largest centralized consumer-product data base of its kind in the world. The data base contains more than 750,000 answers to consumer questions on file. The center receives up to 5 million customer calls each year.

Sharpen Your Selling Strategy

Sharpen your telemarketing strategy by choosing two products (or services) to sell. One product is the primary marketing target, the other the secondary target. Each of the products should offer different advantages. Only promote the secondary item if the primary one doesn't sell.

"Time Line"

The campaign plan starts the process, but a time line (schedule) guides your progress. Assign a date to every function that must be completed (script development, staff training) before the campaign begins. Be sure to revise the time line regularly as you move ahead or fall behind. See the sample time line on page 24.

Project-Team Meeting

Project-team meetings should include all crucial team members (managers, supervisors, trainers, scriptwriters, fulfillment and order-processing staff), and should be held as often as needed before the campaign start date. These meetings afford an opportunity to review crucial dates, and the schedule as a whole. Once the campaign has begun, weekly team meetings are helpful for tracking results, discussing objectives, and monitoring the campaign's progress.

Test the System

Since so many things can go wrong with a computerized "system," which supplies information that management needs to manage and evaluate performance, concentrate your efforts, or your best programmer's time, here. Before a new campaign begins, meet with your operations manager and programmer, and carefully check your procedures. Are reports tabulating correctly? Is data properly flowing to fulfillment? Have you called all the 800 numbers to make sure that they're in working order for the campaign start date?

Measure Objectives

If you don't measure regularly in telemarketing, you can't fix problems. In fact, you won't even know there's a problem. For every new campaign, first determine what you're going to measure, and what these measurements will mean to you. These measurements must be fine-tuned within a short period of time. Use the first week of calling to guide you. You may find that broad objectives can't be achieved. You may establish one set of objectives for frequent buyers, and another set for infrequent buyers.

TIME LINE

CAMPAIGN _____

Activity	Date	Person Responsible
Contract/Service Agreement Signed	_____	_____
Project Team Identified	_____	_____
Project Team Meetings	_____	_____
_____	_____	_____
_____	_____	_____
Script - First Draft	_____	_____
Script - Final Draft	_____	_____
Methods and Procedures First Draft	_____	_____
Methods and Procedures Final Draft	_____	_____
Training - First Draft	_____	_____
Training - Final Draft	_____	_____
Training Schedule Established	_____	_____
Incentive Program - Implemented	_____	_____
Media Start Date/ Mail Drop Date	_____	_____
Campaign Start Date/End Date	_____	_____
Media Material Received (brochures, print ads)	_____	_____
Billing Procedures in Place	_____	_____
Telemarketing Report Sample Due	_____	_____
First Campaign Report Due	_____	_____
Script Testing	_____	_____
Test Calls	_____	_____
Monitoring	_____	_____
End-of-Campaign Analysis (Report)	_____	_____

What if you don't meet your objectives? Your campaign wasn't necessarily a failure. Perhaps your objectives were unrealistically high, or the script may need reworking. Your calling list could have been poor, or the reps weren't properly trained. To achieve the best results, measure—and test again and again.

Track Results

In telemarketing, careful tracking leads to campaign success. Compiling results on an hour-by-hour basis will help you evaluate individual reps, supervisors, lists, scripts, profitability, price, as well as the best days or times to call. Data analysis will also help you to set realistic goals. Reps must be trained to account for every incoming call or outbound dial.

One company has developed a "No-Sale" report listing various reasons why customers don't buy particular services. One advantage of the report is that it tells what the customers want. Consequently, the company is able to improve future services. See the sample report on page 26.

Telemarketing Checklist

Develop a good checklist to help avoid problems in any future campaigns. Develop a checklist for your own telemarketing center by drawing upon your experiences from past campaigns, especially specific problems you may have encountered. Previous promotions can also provide you with basic forms you can reuse, report formats, and quality-control procedures. Note all the important actions you must take, or small details you might easily overlook.

After you have a basic draft, pass around the checklist to everyone you usually work with for their input. Use this checklist routinely every time you start a new campaign, so that all important points are covered before you begin. Key players might approve the document to ensure that everyone holds to his commitments. See the sample checklist on page 27.

Integration

Direct response (or direct mail) coupled with telemarketing can increase sales. Managers often promote one selling strategy in direct response, and a different strategy in the telemarketing script. This confuses the customer when he calls and hears a message from the rep that's different from the one printed in the mail he just received.

Know Your Customers

Before you make your first outbound call, be sure you know who your average customer is. Know your rented list!

At one major telecommunications company, its customers are targeted according to telephone toll usage. Knowing the customer helps sharpen its selling

NO SALE REPORT

Week of _____

Reason	Total
Customer has product/service	_____
Dislikes product/service	_____
Must check with spouse/partner	_____
Doesn't think he'd save money	_____
Wrong person reached	_____
Dislikes company	_____
Has a pending complaint	_____
Decision maker not available	_____
Dislikes telemarketing calls	_____
	Total _____

strategy, refine scripts, and ultimately it benefits its reps, who then know their customers better.

You can never say the word *test* frequently enough in telemarketing. Regularly test new lists against your control list (the list you use now because it's the best to date).

Learn from Your Customers

The next time you monitor your reps, listen carefully to what your customers say. Your customers will tell you whether they want to buy, and they'll also give you reasons why they choose not to buy. Write down their comments, learn from them, and make changes based on these responses.

Take every opportunity to learn more about a caller or person called. Provide a way to retain what you learn to help you plan future promotions. If you don't want to mechanize the data, draw up simple forms to duplicate. Capture customers' unsolicited positive comments as well as their complaints. A "No-Sale" report (mentioned earlier) also provides important data. Categories can range from "doesn't use the service" to "decision-maker not available." These types of reports reveal what's happening in the marketplace.

If you indeed listen closely, customers can tell you which script or list worked best; if the direct-mail piece sent out before the outbound call really helped your

CAMPAIGN FINAL CHECKLIST

CAMPAIGN NAME _____
DATE _____

Campaign Start Date _____   Campaign End Date _____

Script Developed _____   Approved by Legal/
                                    Client   _____

Additional Campaign-Specific Verbiage Completed _____

Estimated Call Volume _____

Report Format Changes _____ Report Testing _____

Daily Reports _____   Weekly Reports_____   Monthly Reports ____

Other Tracking Requirements _____

Objectives:
Average Contact Length _____

Contacts   Completes   Sales
Per Hour _____   Per Hour _____   Per Hour _____

                                                 Conversion
Total Contacts _____   Total Sales _____   Rate _____

Cost Per Sale _____

Number of Attempts to Close _____

Percent of Calls Abandoned _____

Percent of Calls Answered in 20 Seconds _____

Monitoring Schedule Developed _____

Percent of Calls to be Monitored _____

Percent of Calls Monitored Considered
Excellent/Satisfactory _____

Customer Satisfaction Rating _____

System Tested _____

Campaign Data Definitions Defined/Documented_____

Tapes _____
(Containing Prospect Names, Telephone #)

Rep Training   Methods and   Rep Job Aids
Package Developed _____   Procedures Done _____   Completed _____

Training Schedule Done _____   #Reps to Train _____

Media Schedule (Direct Mail and Print Ad Drop Dates) _____

Media Material (brochures, direct mail) Received _____

---

800 # Checked _____

Campaign Estimate _____   Campaign Final Bill _____

End-of-Campaign Report Due _____

Additional Requirements _____

---

rep sell the product; or, which brought in more calls—the radio or TV commercial, or the print ad.

Scripts

Poor scripts can bedevil your campaign. Avoid problems by using simple, everyday words. Direct-mail copy won't work in scripts. Conversational dialogue *will* work.

A good script will help the rep control the call. Without control, average talk time increases, and so do costs. You won't know if your new script is giving you the highest return unless you test two scripts. Again, testing and telemarketing go together. Track sales and customer reaction from both scripts.

Information Screens

Never allow reps to improvise a response to customers' questions. The end result will be inconsistencies, omissions, and poor call quality. With your computer programmer, develop general information screens, question-and-answer screens, and rebuttal screens to ensure consistent replies to consumers' questions. If your center isn't mechanized, print this information on reference cards, or place it in binders.

A set script is especially important for warranties, guarantees, payment descriptions, liabilities, and regulatory information. Cut down on faulty purchases by fully describing the features of your products, and how the customer will be billed.

Keep Current to Help Credibility

Sometimes it's easy to forget the things that aren't giving you any trouble. Set up a schedule to regularly review all scripts, general information computer screens, question-and-answer computer screens, rebuttal screens, product/service screens, reps' binders, training materials, brochures, direct-mail pieces, form letters, catalogs, and commercials. Keep track of start/end dates for special offers.

Most important, when you change your prices, or strategy, or you add new products, be sure to review all the material mentioned above.

Your company's internal reports and forms must also be regularly reviewed at least once a year, and preferably every six months. Do the forms still fit your needs? Can reports be simplified? Can two reports be combined into one?

Anyone having a stake in the report should be on the revision committee. To save costs, complete this process when you're running out of your current forms.

Hiring Telephone Sales Representatives

Spend a little extra time when hiring, and you'll reap the benefits later on. Your first interview with the applicant should be on the telephone. This technique simulates the conditions of the job, and is a form of role-play. Important traits to listen for include a clear, well-modulated voice, sincerity, and patience. The applicant should also be a good listener.

During the second interview, emphasize motivation, teamwork, participation, and quality.

Hire employees with the understanding that theirs isn't just another part-time job. Experience shows that 4 to 5 hours of outbound telemarketing sustains call productivity and prevents employee burnout.

Training/Keeping Telephone Sales Representatives

Provide your reps with in-depth training about your products/services. Your reps should know your products inside out, and they should also understand your company's business philosophy. Strive to make your reps a true part of your team. Emphasize how important the reps' ideas and suggestions are to you. You get your best ideas from reps—all you have to do is listen to them.

Offer your employees compensation plans, career paths, and goals. Don't resign yourself to high turnover and unmotivated reps. Provide your staff with the proper facilities so that they have enough space to do their work. Don't put work stations so close together that customers can hear other reps in the background.

Regular coaching and monitoring of your reps contributes to their development, and to the success of your business.

Staffing Techniques for Inbound Calls

Staffing for direct-response TV (promotional commercials urging customers to call an 800 number to place an order) differs greatly from staffing for outbound calling. Use past inbound-calling history to predict responses, and to avoid low accessibility (percentage of calls handled within a certain time) and high abandonment rate (calls that never reach a rep, usually hang-ups due to caller impatience). During heavy calling periods, utilize an "automated voice response system" (equipment or service that answers calls and invites the caller to respond to a series of prompts to route him to the proper department). Maintain a list of "reps on call" to help you on heavy calling days.

Campaign Kickoff

Before a new campaign begins, someone will ask if you really need a "kickoff." You *need* a kickoff to create excitement, and to make the reps feel that they're a part of the team.

At your kickoffs, explain to the reps the details of the promotion, and the campaign/sales strategy. Give each rep a sales kit containing the mail piece, or print ads, and your strategy statements. If a commercial was developed, have the reps watch it on videotape. Decorate the center, serve refreshments, and give a small gift to each rep.

Your Data Base

A data base is a collection of information about each customer who has in some way responded to the product/service offered by a company. Customers are those who've responded by telephone or by mail. "Qualified buyers" are those who've spent money on your product. "Inquirers" are those who've shown some interest in your product. They may have requested a free catalog, for example.

Benefits of data-base marketing

Gather customer information to help you identify your target market. Whether you target consumers or businesses, data such as product preference, revenue/income level, as well as other information can help you develop future marketing plans. You'll be able to respond to customer needs based on what they tell you when you're gathering data. The more you know about your customers, the better your data base, and the better you'll be able to use it.

Build your customer data base

A data base that's useful to your company isn't something you can acquire quickly. Build your data base slowly, testing, retesting, expanding, and testing again the best methods of acquiring names and other related information.

To build your data base, first examine your data-base needs and write them down. Be specific. Next, translate these needs into dollar benefits. Separate the "need to know" information from the "nice to have" information. Design your management reports first by bringing together a team (from all levels of personnel) from the appropriate departments. Incorporate their reporting needs into your final plan.

The basic types of data-base information to collect include: general information such as name, address, customer code, purchase history, source of customer name, first purchase, items purchased, sizes, money spent, number of purchases, returns, date of last purchase, and credit information.

Other information to gather includes promotions history, number of individual catalogs mailed, number of mailings, service history. Use this data to evaluate dollar value and quality of each customer, type of customer complaints, customer-service reports, and miscellaneous data such as address changes, customer research, best customers, sources providing the best return (mail, telephone), cost to promote.

Enhance your data base

When you combine a customer's purchase history and other data with the depth of information available through a telemarketing contact, you build a marketing resource that becomes increasingly more valuable.

There are other ways to add value to your data base. Keep your data base dynamic, ever changing and up-to-date. Maintain data on former, current, and new customers. Analyze all data on mail, telemarketing, and field-sales efforts. Record literature and catalog requests.

Sometimes, especially for smaller telemarketing centers, it may be less expensive to use an outside vendor than to build and maintain a computerized data base. Outside contractors usually have software that's more sophisticated than many developed in-house. Choose an approach that works for your center.

Sell a Product or Service Over the Telephone

When you develop your script and campaign, take a few minutes to put yourself in your customer's place. He has virtually no visual aid to identify the product or service you sell. Maybe he can form a hazy vision in his mind about your product. But if you're selling a service, he may be bewildered by something that has neither form nor shape. Make it easy for your customer by painting vivid pictures with colorful words to describe the benefits of your product or service. Reps should project a positive, enthusiastic tone by using friendly words. Tone of voice and speed of conversation should vary. Capitalize on the personal nature of the medium to win customers.

Separate Sales from Service

Effectively utilize your reps' talents by separating service calls from sales calls. Reps who like to sell will be able to, and reps who enjoy customer service can do just that. When you separate the two applications, your telemarketing center will run better.

Determine Telemarketing Costs

To determine an average cost per call, use "loaded" costs which include office overhead, data processing and other system costs, and labor. Refer to the following checklist to determine your costs.

- Script development
- Training materials and instruction
- Development of methods and procedures
- Reps' salaries
- Reps' work space
- Equipment
- Local and long-distance telephone usage

- Supervisors' salaries
- List rental
- Advertisements (print, direct-mail, catalog, broadcast/cable)
- Fulfillment costs

Telemarketing Sales Cycle

Telemarketing offers an effective and complete sales cycle because it provides communication, and quick feedback and response. The cycle begins with the direct-mail drop. The customer prospect is then called and qualified. More information is mailed or a price quote is offered. A closed call makes the sale. A confirmation and a thank-you letter are sent. The customer is later called to determine if he's satisfied with the product. Follow-up information is mailed, and the close completes another cycle.

Tie-In Sales

To increase your sales, tie your product or service to an upcoming holiday. Create urgency by offering the promotion for a limited time.

"Sign up for our service and you'll save money on your long-distance holiday calls."

Maintain a Team Vision

Employees who've participated in the implementation of a new campaign should be told how their contributions resulted in your organization meeting major milestones. Gather a group together and give a short presentation on total revenue generated by the campaign, emphasizing the areas where expectations were exceeded, or new approaches that were successful. Use posters to display these achievements, and hang the posters on walls, where everyone can bask in the glory of the successful campaign. Allow employees to monitor their progress towards their own individual objectives.

Sourcebook of Common Information

Create a sourcebook of common information customized to your center's needs. The book should contain the things you seem to forget at times, but that you need to know to effectively manage the center. Examples include: date of next promotion, mailing dates, acceptable abandonment rates, conversion rates for different campaigns, average length of inbound/outbound calls, cost of individual products. Develop an index for all the subjects in the binder. Appoint a team of reps to determine the subject matter of the book; they know best what the binder should contain.

What Do Customers Want?

Meeting customers' expectations should be an important part of your telemarketing program. Customer service never really ends. Reps should ask customers questions and listen carefully to their responses. Train your reps to gather information by recording customers' unsolicited responses, both positive and negative, as well as customers' suggestions. Implement outbound telephone surveys, but always tell customers what you'll be doing with the results of the survey so the customers won't feel that you're wasting their time. A survey can help your sales and service departments to better meet customer requirements.

Your reps' communication style should also be appropriate to what the customer expects: Formality? Familiarity? A rep versed in the technical language of the client?

Help Reps Sell—Fulfillment

The calls keep coming in, but the products aren't yet ready to be sent out. Providing both customer satisfaction and fulfillment in a timely manner requires that all sales kits, brochures, and literature be ready by the start of the campaign. Accomplish this task by making one person responsible for tracking the fulfillment schedule.

Make sure that your reps have a copy of every print ad, brochure, or direct-mail piece. Too often, customers refer to a particular ad, but the rep doesn't know anything about it because he's never seen it. Give your reps current promotional pieces to make them part of the team, and to increase their confidence. If they need to, they can read along with the customers on the telephone to better clarify the offer. This promotes a trusting relationship with customers.

Always closely coordinate your direct-mail drop date with your outbound calling so that customers receive the mail before the calls.

A Reason for Every Call

You must have a legitimate reason to call customers—informing customers of a special sales price or offer, conducting a survey, or introducing your firm.

Maintain a Good Service Level

When a center handles a large volume of calls per rep, the result may be poor service. Don't increase the center's calls per day—you may jeopardize service level. You'll pay dearly when reps handle too many calls. A good service level can result in lower employee turnover and decrease "burnout."

Complex Campaigns

Many times an organization is faced with a complex campaign, perhaps a type of campaign that's never been done before. Surprisingly, these are the campaigns that teach you the most.

Tactics to handle complex campaigns include setting specific objectives for the campaign, holding frequent team meetings to review the campaign's progress (and making the necessary adjustments), identifying problems early on, and implementing procedures to correct the problems.

Other techniques include developing a customized training package that addresses the campaign's peculiarities, and writing a completely new script for the campaign. If the project is done on paper, do "quality checks" of the documentation. Create a flowchart of the entire process so you don't miss crucial operational steps. Organize your reps in working teams to handle special requirements.

Designate supervisors to be responsible for the end-to-end processing of activities in their groups. Script all possible customer objections and appropriate rebuttals (to present opposing evidence to a customer's objections). Write out difficult procedures in a format a rep can easily follow.

Document typical problems and frequent complaints to help you in subsequent campaigns. If a rep or his supervisor can't answer a question, arrange to call the customer back. File all reports on campaign data for possible future reference. When the campaign ends, draw up a final "end-of-campaign" report. This is a good document to provide to top management and clients. It also provides a valuable blueprint for similar upcoming campaigns.

Create a "Look" for Your Campaign

Give your promotion a distinctive name that "rings a bell" every time your customer comes across it, in any medium.

A distinctive logo can appear on all your promotions, products, and literature. A company "look" can make a positive, memorable impression, especially if you consistently incorporate the "look" in all your media.

Gain Acceptance for Your Forms

Tracking forms and reports will be more readily accepted if you seek input from other departments during the design phase. Consider your reps' suggestions, too. Team input makes for a good document, the result being complete correct data.

Don't Underestimate the Importance of the Center's Environment

In the hectic atmosphere of a telemarketing center, sometimes it's easy for managers to focus on the crisis of the moment without paying too much attention to the physical and psychological environment. Neglecting these environmental aspects can make a center lose its vitality.

When you first enter your telemarketing center, try to forget how well you know this building and its interior. Imagine that you're a rep working here, or a prospective client coming to the office for the first time. What do you see? Spotted, faded posters, dreary walls, peeling paint, unkempt bathrooms, clutter, worn carpets, dirty windows, dusty shelves, drooping plants? Even a few of the above examples project a strong message. What does this environment tell your reps about your company? How does the work area make reps feel? Depressed? Warm? Comfortable? Spruce up your center and reap the benefits.

Provide an inviting physical environment, and cultivate a good emotional environment. Create an environment where reps can share their successes. After making a sale or dealing with a difficult customer, encourage reps to immediately share their experiences with someone. When a rep talks about a success right after it occurs, it helps him to better retain those skills that brought the success, and such interactions may spur others on to success.

The GE Answer Center operates on a "face-to-face" concept. Reps are encouraged to behave as if they were face-to-face with the customer. The offices are designed for teamwork and privacy. GE aims to build a bond with the customer so that he believes that GE's rep *is* indeed GE. Managers will often move employees to different work stations as a way to change the scenery and lower stress.

Enhance Your Telemarketing Center

Once your telemarketing center is up and running, your next challenge is to enhance your center's functions. You might add one of the following functions. You could centralize incoming and outgoing telemarketing operations, or you could follow up leads with outgoing calls. Suppress bad credit and duplicates. Track dollars spent on advertising against total sales for each channel to help you determine your cost per media.

Troubleshooting is simply a good management skill. Before a campaign even begins, ensure that you have sufficient inventory and staff to handle orders. Since there's no way to guarantee that a telemarketing program will be successful and cost-effective, always pretest various segments of your target audience, and choose the most lucrative segments. Any change in your campaign goals will change the role of your telemarketing operation. Supply new reps with a list of your company's acronyms and a glossary, so that they understand your organization's language. Telemarketing management is not an exact science with steadfast principles; you must continually accommodate change. Always be prepared at the earliest stage for any problem that can happen. Keep a program going by using good precampaign planning and developing well-thought-out policies and procedures. This prevents unexpected crises and tedious double-checking. Consider all associated costs when planning your program.

If a last-minute change has occurred, broadcast it on an information screen on the reps' computer terminals, or distribute a paper copy to the reps. Distribute changes quickly so that your reps will be well informed. When planning a new campaign, develop a new incentive program, too, to keep reps motivated. If you alter one aspect of the campaign during the planning stages, check the impact on other aspects. Any changes made in direct-mail pieces should be reflected in your script, for example.

Anticipate customers' responses by preparing scripted rebuttals for your reps. Give your reps regular feedback on calls, or they may keep repeating the same mistakes. As you write a script for a new campaign, imagine that you're the customer, with nothing to touch or see of what the rep is selling. Keep a new program dynamic by regularly monitoring, revising, and updating your marketing and campaign plans based on market feedback and results. Install separate 800 numbers for your sales and service calls. Otherwise, every time a service call comes in, it could block a sales call.

Make Telemarketing Work for You

When testing a new campaign, use two different scripts to determine which one gives you the best results. Use the winner in your campaign. Highlight your inbound 800 number on all promotions. If you use a vanity (alpha) 800 number, print the corresponding numbers for easy dialling (e.g., 1-800-KLUTSES, 1-800-558-8737). Identify your target audience before you begin calling.

If you sell a service, send out a confirmation letter after processing the order, and tell the customer you're doing so. Otherwise, things could fall through the cracks, and both you and the customer might think that the order has been processed. Train your reps to always record impromptu customer comments. These comments could alert you to campaign needs, concerns, or ideas for new products. Take time to analyze this data. What does it tell you? Promote any changes you make that benefit the customer directly *to* the customer. Boast about your easy ordering process, your customer-service department, and your knowledgeable reps.

Always test, but test one factor at a time during a campaign: script, lists, sales message, media, direct-mail package, and training module. Create opportunities for your inside-sales and outside-sales employees to meet face-to-face, thereby building upon their business relationship. Some opportunities include sales recognition events, conferences, or new product kickoffs. All telemarketing reps sound alike to customers. Try to make your reps sound better. Empower your supervisors to interview, hire, train, and manage their teams. Encourage inside- and outside-sales employees to work as a team by asking them to put together an informational booklet on communications—who's responsible for what. This booklet could be used as part of an orientation package for new employees. Maintain an updated list of all the brochures available to customers, or create a brochure portfolio (with actual brochure samples) for reps to browse through.

Remember to praise. This is a skill frequently forgotten by managers. This motivation can affect behavior more quickly than other methods. If you recently developed a new training package, test it on a small class before using it routinely.

Inbound

Pose a one- or two-sentence suggestion when cross-selling (suggesting that the customer buy an additional item that's related to the one he just purchased). On inbound calls, be sure that the cross-sell offer directly relates to the order being placed. Get free research data from a proven purchaser. Ask your customer what aspect of the product prompted him to order it. Always deliver a marketing message with your shipment. Send a bounce-back order form promoting your other products, and a thank-you note. Cross-sell during customer-service calls. The customer may have a need for a related product or service. Cross-sell in a nonaggressive manner. Always ask the caller for the source of an order or inquiry in order to track the effectiveness of advertising media. Make your offers clear to avoid expensive calls from prospects seeking clarification of your print ad or commercial.

Educate your customer in your literature. Say where to call for orders, and where to call for customer service. You'll avoid wasted 800-number calls. During an incoming call, ask one or two questions to help your future marketing efforts. However, don't do a full questionnaire. Verify the customer's name and address at the beginning and at the end of the sales call. By doing this, you'll noticeably cut down on errors. Customers rarely complain about the second verification request.

Train your reps to "brand" each call at the end: "Thank you for using AT&T." This leaves the customer with a good feeling and keeps your company name on his mind. Distribute direct-mail pieces to reps before the campaign begins, so they can refer to them during calls. If a customer gives you a name or address correction during the call, get this change into the computer system immediately. You risk customer irritation if you don't. Tell the customer if his order is in stock. Be "easy-to-do-business with" and transfer customer calls instead of giving another number to call. Regularly track "market intelligence"—the unsolicited but valuable comments your customers make during the course of a call. One company has implemented a special program to track these comments, including forms to record the information, as well as an incentive program for reps. Use this data to help solve problems.

Outbound

Teach reps to give their presentations concisely and in a low-key manner. Deliver your message through print or mail, and then have your reps call. Write scripted rebuttals so your company delivers one message. Use screening questions (a series of questions reps use to determine if the person he's speaking with is an appropriate prospect for the product) to properly qualify customers. Record reactions to the features of your product, its pricing, or any customer comments about your competitors. Probe for purchase interest, but train reps to "know" when to terminate the call. Follow leads promptly; customers forget quickly.

Make outbound calls one to two weeks after your direct-mail drop. Train reps to determine early in the call who the decision-maker is. Be specific when arranging callback times with customers. Avoid calling customers twice in one week.

2
TRAINING AND HIRING

Spend extra time hiring and training, and you'll get good results. Turn away from the myth that high turnover in telemarketing is inevitable. Once you eliminate random hiring practices, turnover will decline. Reject the idea that you can survive merely with warm bodies. The cost of quick turnover and low productivity results in high costs to the company. If you calculate the cost of just one low-producing rep occupying one of your work stations, your attitude will change.

Get your hiring practices in order. Raise your expectations and standardize your procedures so that you always attract the same type of prospect. This approach will also save you time. Build a "prospect success" file so you know which attributes you're looking for. What traits should a top rep have? Interview more prospects than usual, but be more selective in your choice of interviewees. Develop an interview format, and give candidates a realistic overview of the job. If one hiring approach doesn't work, try to determine why, and then correct the problem area. Or, try another tactic.

The difference between *good* companies and *excellent* companies is training. Excellent training lays a solid foundation for all the business interactions that follow. When it comes to telemarketing, companies tend to give the field-sales staff extensive training, while the inside-sales staff may be given only a few days of training. Reverse this process by thinking of training as an investment, rather than as a cost. Top management must accept this view, as well. You can't spend too much money on training. Tom Peters agrees: "No firm I know has ever overtrained sales, service, and support people. And make sure it's the right kind of training."

Maintain a focused approach. If you train a customer-service rep, focus on building relationships with the customers, rather than concentrating on computer skills.

Training should be ongoing; do it every day, and in every possible way. Help your reps to view training as a positive part of their daily job. Don't let training turn into a "fix it when it's broke" activity. Ongoing training should *add* to the knowledge that your reps already have.

Create a climate for learning and growth. A telemarketing center should recognize creative thinking and the use of skills that bring success. Supervisors should become coaches, praising and reinforcing behaviors they want their reps to repeat.

The following pages provide some information to use when hiring and training reps. These "starting points" need to be adapted and added to before you get the right employees for your company. These tips should provide you with a never-ending cycle of revitalization for your company. Step back to review and revise your hiring practices. Be ready with some new retraining techniques almost as soon as your new employees leave the classroom. Your own unique ideas will also multiply the benefits.

Before You Write the Job Description

Ask yourself these questions to enable you to write a clear job description, and to determine the type of applicant you're seeking. How does telemarketing fit into the company's marketing plan? Will the reps supplement the efforts of the field-sales force? Is the primary purpose of the job to respond to direct mail, or to direct-response television? Is the function of the job to find, qualify, and close leads? Will the reps do "cold" calls, or will they provide customer service? Will the reps be selling one product to a single market, or will they be offering a multiple-product line to different types of markets?

Will the average sale be low-dollar volume or high-dollar volume? Will the reps be selling existing products or newly introduced products? Who makes the buying decisions? How complex is the sales process? Is my company well known? Must the rep first develop the company image?

Writing the Job Description

Before you place an ad in the newspaper, you must write the job description. The rep's job description should contain the following information.

- Job title
- Name of the manager to whom the employee will report
- A short paragraph explaining the main function of the job
- Detailed information on the nature and scope of the job including functions to be performed by the incumbent, major challenges of the position, level of authority of the position, problems and actions that need to be passed upwards for solution, necessary contacts within the company to successfully complete job responsibilities, explanation of how job performance will be measured (including monitoring/taping for training purposes), background required, experience, knowledge and training needed for satisfactory job performance, responsibilities of the position listed in numerical order. State exactly what's expected of the employee.

A well-written and -developed job description will help you hire the best candidate, provide clear information to the employee about job requirements, and provide a clear format when you're ready to write the employee's performance appraisal, since the goals and objectives for performance are clearly defined.

Ad Placement

Do	**Don't**
Place your ad under sales, customer communications, or the general name of your industry.	Place your ad under telephone sales, telemarketing, or miscellaneous.
Place your ad in the classified section of local regional newspapers or trade publications.	Place your ad in out-of-town newspapers. Applicants and new hires might find commuting difficult.

Write the Ad

Stick to the basics, and forget the flowery phrases. "Sell" the benefits of the job, emphasizing the knowledge the reps will acquire, the opportunities for advancement, and the independence the reps will have. One headline might read, "You could be our next success story." Emphasize the job skills required. If you are primarily interested in sales, write that you're "looking for closers." Boast about a complete benefits package and the opportunities for bonuses.

Interview your top reps. Ask them what they like about their current jobs. Advertise these aspects to attract more of the same type of rep.

Go one step further. Put pictures of your top reps and their endorsements in the newspaper. This approach tells your current employees that their jobs are important to you, and it will make them feel good.

Some managers believe that small ads attract part-time, short-term employees, and that the bigger the ad the more important the message. Others think several smaller ads work better than one big one. Which approach should you try? You won't know which works best for you until you test both. Track the results of your ads to tell you which ads are most effective. This also helps you control costs. Ask each applicant where he saw your ad, and record these responses in a log. Run ads only in those newspapers that give you top results.

Save time by requesting that applicants send résumés. A quick review of these résumés will help you eliminate those candidates who don't meet the minimum qualifications.

Use other channels to recruit reps. Use college bulletin boards, or bulletin boards in stores in your community. Accept referrals from your current employees. Offer your employees a cash bounty for every applicant they recommend who stays for three months.

Hold job fairs and publicize them beforehand. Place an ad in residential coupon mail packs to reach those prospects who might not read the classifieds, or those who aren't actively looking for a job. You may need to try the coupon mail packs more than once, to be able to create awareness of your company and to emphasize the opportunities in telemarketing.

Print recruitment cards, about the same size as standard business cards. Have the card read, "Cash award for successful commissioned salesperson. To join a winning team, call now." Have your managers and employees hand them out. Prepare an informational article (or get your local newspaper to write an article) about your company. Explain the opportunities available in telemarketing, and describe what the job entails. When the article is published, make glossy reprints of it and distribute them to your employees, customers, and local colleges. Give copies to interviewees.

Advertise regularly. The cumulative results will be amazing. Prospects may watch an ad for weeks before applying for a job.

What to Look for in a Rep

Look for these characteristics when you interview a prospect by telephone: clear, distinct, pleasant voice, natural speech (at a rate of 120–145 words per minute), simple straightforward language, ability to convey personality and emotion about what he says through voice alone, enthusiasm, confidence, positive attitude, good communications skills, and good grammar.

Look for these characteristics when you interview a prospect in person: enjoys working on the phone, common sense, good work record, functions well under pressure, empathetic, likes people, good listening skills, "thick skinned," good penmanship and spelling, good typing skills, some exposure to computers, willing to work weekends and evenings, persistent, and able to copy and repeat accurately.

Telephone Interview

The telephone interview really begins the hiring process. Don't let prospects apply in person. Use the telephone to screen out unsuitable applicants. To maintain consistency and provide yourself with guidelines, use a telephone-interview form each time you talk with a prospect. See page 43. Before calling the applicant, review his résumé. During the call, briefly describe the job in four or five sentences. Use this screening call to judge the applicant's communication skills, vocabulary, and voice quality. Is there a "smile" in the sound of the candidate's voice? Since a rep can only "tell" and not show, does he have the ability to select words that generate positive mental images?

How does the candidate handle the call? Judge the applicant's interest in the job, and clarify points on the résumé. If you're satisfied with the telephone screening, schedule an in-person interview. Only 75% of the people you invite will actually show up for the in-person interview.

In-Person Interview

During the in-person interview, stick to a consistent set of questions. This ensures that you'll cover all the important topics required to judge the candidate. Established criteria will also help you quickly weed out ineligible applicants.

When the candidate arrives, have him fill out a job application. Check the

Today's Date: _____   Face-to-Face Interview:
                                              Date:_____
                                              Time:_____

Telephone Sales Representative
Telephone Interview

I'm sure you have some questions about the job, but first let me
ask you some basic questions about yourself.

o   Name _____   o   Phone _____
o   Address _____
o   City _____   o   State _____   o   Zip Code _____
o   How long at this address? _____
o   How far is that in driving time from our Company? _____
    _____
o   Last Job _____   o   Length of service _____
o   Pay at last job _____   o
o   Number of employers within last five years _____
o   Skills _____
o   Have you ever been in sales? _____
o   Do you like to talk on the phone? _____
o   Can you type? _____   o   Computer literate? _____
o   Quality of phone voice _____
o   Enthusiasm _____   o   Confidence _____
o   Are you interested in part-time work? _____
                         o   full-time work? _____
o   Can you work weekends? _____
o   Evenings? _____
o   The starting pay is _____ per hour
o   Would that be acceptable? _____
o   The job involves speaking with (business people) (consumers)
    over the telephone. Does this sound like something you
    might be interested in? _____

o   If the prospect isn't acceptable:
    Thank you for your interest in the job, but we're looking for
    people with more _____ experience.
                       work/sales/phone

o   If the prospect is acceptable:
    You sound like the kind of person we're looking for. Can
    you come in for an interview? _____
    Date _____   Time _____

o   Comments: _____
    _____
    _____

o   Telephone Interview by   _____

completed form to see if he correctly followed your directions. Talk to the candidate about the products he'll be selling. Emphasize the intensity of the job, giving the applicant a realistic idea of the work to be done. Be sure to ask open-ended questions: "Why do you want this job?" "Tell me about yourself." While the applicant talks, judge communications skills, how he structures his conversation, and how he uses language. Were your judgments about the applicant during the telephone interview the same as they are now? Is the applicant a positive representative for your company? Can you work with this person?

At this point, many managers end the interview and set up another appointment to include testing and role-plays.

There are several reasons for using the second in-person interview. It indicates to the applicant that you're selective. Sometimes this tactic makes your company more appealing to applicants. A second interview lets you test a candidate's dependability. If you have an urgent need for reps, you may have to combine the two in-person interviews.

Second In-Person Interview

During this interview, test the applicant's ability to follow oral and written instructions. Role-play should range from very simple calls to very challenging situations, when the rep must deal with hostility. Test the applicant's ability to do more than one thing at a time and test his concentration by creating some distraction during the role-playing.

At one telemarketing center, applicants are provided with "case study" role-plays. They're given time to prepare their calls, and then they use the phone to "sell" managers on the other end.

Later, take applicants on a tour of your telemarketing center so that they can get a feel for the work environment.

Teamwork Is Important

Typically, reps work with a group of people doing the same tasks. There's usually a need for the team members to help each other. These teams have group goals and incentives. Evaluate each candidate's ability to work as part of a team. The best indicator of future success is past performance. Get the names and phone numbers of the applicant's supervisors from his two previous jobs, and talk with them about the candidate.

Pre-In-Person Interview Test

Make it easy for applicants to learn something about your company before you interview them. Leave brochures and copies of your catalogs in the reception room. Hang framed reprints and clippings of newspaper and magazine stories about your company and its projects. See if any of the candidates mention any of the products or printed information they've seen.

Is Experience Necessary?

Previous experience may be a hindrance if the applicant has developed poor telephone-sales techniques or habits.

Employee Contracts

Employee contracts contain a detailed agreement of what's fair and reasonable for both parties. The contract should contain a list of the rep's responsibilities, the terms of employment, information about compensation and termination, employee benefits, a section on restricted material (proprietary, trade secrets, mailing lists, research, confidential information), a clause on monitoring (see chapter 3), and cross-training responsibilities.

Exit Interview

Conduct an exit interview to determine why employees leave your company, especially if you have high turnover. This information may correct the turnover problem. Include these questions in the exit interview: Lack of job knowledge? Not enough training? Low wages? Poor work environment?

Before Preparing Your Training

According to Robert W. Pike, author of *Creative Training Techniques Handbook*, the key to an outstanding training program is proper preparation. Pike prescribes six "Ps": "Proper preparation and practice prevent poor performance." Your training is only as good as your preparation and your upkeep of the program. Keep the following points in mind as you develop training.

Establish your objectives

Break down your broad objectives into smaller ones. As a result of this training, how will employees greet customers? How will they determine customers' needs? Will they feel self-confident about their skills? What do they need to know? How will training results be measured? By defining specific smaller goals, it's easier to attain them.

Assess current status

What past experience and knowledge do new employees bring to their training? What are they expecting? What's the average talk time and sales of the current reps? Answering these questions will help you set standards for the future.

Develop a training outline

The longer and more complex your training is, the more you'll need to introduce variety and a change of pace. David A. Peoples, who wrote *Presentations Plus*, claims people gain 75% of what they know visually, 13% through hearing, and 12% through smell, touch, and taste. Words and pictures together are six times more valuable for retention and comprehension than are words alone. The best approach is to stimulate the whole student. Do this in a variety of ways. Bring in subject-matter experts both from inside and from outside your company. Alternate theory with time on the phones. Regularly revitalize your program with new training techniques.

Make sure you plan bridging activities as you move from one subject area to the next. Encourage your students to ask themselves what the single most important idea they've learned is. What will they do with this idea?

Ideas for training adults

Desire Adults must *want* to learn. Adults learn best when they're strongly motivated either to acquire a skill or to increase their knowledge. The desired benefit provides the motivation. Create the desire to learn by emphasizing the importance of the task and the benefits to be derived from doing it.

Need Adults learn only when they feel a *need* to learn. Materials should provide an immediate benefit to the student's work or personal environment.

Learning by doing Comprehending and knowing what to do are not enough in themselves. *Applying* the knowledge is necessary. Provide the students with immediate and repeated opportunities to practise what they learn. On-the-job training with a skilled coach is the most effective way to help retain new learning.

Realism The work situations discussed in class should be believable and important. Use actual situations as the basis for the lesson. Students can use situations from their own experience.

Previous experience Adults need to relate what they're learning to what they already know. Learners usually reject new learning that doesn't fit in with what they already know.

Environment Adults learn best in a relaxed and informal environment. Provide opportunities for fun and fellowship. Encourage discussion and questions. Avoid arguments that relate to your company's policies.

Variety Adults soon become bored with the same methods. Change the pace often. Try new materials and approaches to keep fresh.

Guidance Provide help, not grades nor evaluations.

Training suggestions

As you begin training, tell your reps that their input is important. From the first day of training, cultivate an atmosphere that encourages reps to share their ideas and suggestions. To encourage team effort, let them know that their input is important.

Supervisors are coaches. They're there to support and to motivate reps, and to answer their questions and concerns. Supervisors should work with their reps to help them develop career paths in the center.

Emphasize that the ideas learned in training are the real ideas that exist in your center today. Then be sure to go ahead and practise what you preach.

Put monitoring in its proper place. To new employees, monitoring is threatening. Present monitoring as a tool used by supervisors to guide and support employees, and it will become more palatable.

During training, encourage students to keep an "action idea" list. On this list, trainees should jot down all useful ideas they learn that they can apply on the job. Review these lists with the group at the end of training. Share the best ideas.

At the GE Answer Center, reps are trained to respond to a customer within the first ten seconds of a call according to the customer's personality type. For example, if a customer sounds anxious or insecure, the reps are taught to assume the role of a nurturing parent, reassuring the customer and generating a sense of calm and order. The seven caller personalities and their corresponding "response personalities" are listed below. Role-play these personalities with your trainees.

Caller Personality	Response Personality
Direct/natural	Efficient, confident, and pleasant
Pleasant/outgoing	Pleasant, outgoing, friendly, exchanging a bit of small talk
Insecure/anxious	Nurturing parent, reassuring, generating a sense of well-being
Confused/uncertain	Patient, caring, clarifying
Angry/belligerent	Empathetic listening, responding positively with understanding and follow-through
Urgent/panicked	Equal amount of urgency in dialogue, and in proposing action
Skeptical/cynical	Reassuring, knowledgeable response

A Businesslike Voice

Your voice projects an image over the telephone. Listed below are the attributes of a businesslike voice.

Appropriate volume Speak into the telephone as you would speak to someone two or three feet away. Varying the volume adds interest for the listener and brings out key points.

Clarity This comes from correct pronunciation. Open your mouth wide as you frame your words. Avoid lazy habits, such as trailing off at the end of sentences, or slurring over syllables in the middle of words. Use crisp-sounding words and emphasize them with pauses.

Tone This conveys a strong message to the listener. Sincerity and enthusiasm can be communicated as clearly as the negative tones of phoniness, pushiness, or boredom. Communicate a positive attitude by smiling. We know (without seeing their faces) when people smile as they speak on the telephone. Tone often communicates your meaning better than your words.

Speed This is also an indicator of attitude, according to most listeners. Speaking at a rate of 150–160 words per minute is considered ideal. Speak any faster, and the listener will doubt your credibility. Speak any slower, and the listener will get bored.

Evaluate a Rep's Voice

Use the chart below to evaluate your reps' voices.

Volume	too soft	varied
	too loud	
Clarity	slurred	crisp
Tone	timid	confident
	phony	sincere
	bored	enthusiastic
	pushy	
Speed	too slow	good pace
	too fast	

Requests and Opportunities

Incoming messages to your business are always opportunities. Each type of incoming message listed below presents a variety of opportunities; all enable you to sell products and services.

Customer complaints Save an important customer. Do a better job in the future.

Suggestions from the public Increase customer loyalty.

Information requests Determine needs.

Order placement Add to the order.

Service requests Respond efficiently to the immediate problem.

Mail inquiries Analyze for clues about reasons and needs. Do pre-call preparation.

Telephone inquiries Identify yourself, listen, express interest, and offer your help. Record inquirer information, answer the inquiry or arrange for a return call.

Train Reps to Listen

Many people hear only a portion of what's said to them, especially on the telephone. They listen for key words and phrases to give them the main point of the conversation. They fill in the gaps with their own thoughts or what they think will be said. The trainer has two challenges to face. Train the reps to be good listeners, and teach them how to gain their customers' attention.

Follow these steps to train good listeners. Reps are responsible for their half of the communication; they should have their own objectives in mind while determining the speaker's purpose. They should listen for the main idea and ask questions as needed. Reps must also limit their own talk. They should think like customers to better understand customer needs and concerns. They should think in pictures, take notes, concentrate on the customers' words, and repeat questions and statements back to the customer. Reps should react to the *ideas* they hear, not to the customer's personality. The customer's irritation shouldn't distract the rep. The rep should never interrupt. The rep must hear out the customer-prospect. He shouldn't mentally argue with the customer while he's talking; he'll distract himself. The rep should show the customer that he's listening carefully, using occasional interjections, "Yes," "I understand." However, the rep shouldn't overdo it. Good listening also involves getting customers to talk more about their objections so reps can determine the customers' real motivations. Reps can never assume anything, or answer questions for the prospects. Of course, they should occasionally agree with customers in order to show that they're interested in what's being said.

To get customers to listen to them, reps should use expression, speed of voice, and rhythm to give their voices flavor and gusto. Using buzz words can also arouse and motivate the listener. Enthusiasm is contagious! Not only does it get the customer's attention, but it also creates interest. The basis for enthusiasm is confidence, and confidence is made up of knowledge and attitude.

Role-Play

According to the *Encyclopedia of Telemarketing,*

> Role-play is a training technique in which trainees have the opportunity to take turns playing the telemarketing rep and the prospect. By actually talking with a "customer," reps learn what to say and how to say it, getting experience communicating with your market before they actually have to get on the telephone with customers.

Here are the basic rules of role-play. Determine the training objective for every role-play. Decide which skills will be taught or improved. Share the purpose of the role-play with your group. Develop situations that incorporate challenges that reps face daily: objections, closing a sale, irate customers. Keep role-play groups small. Put a time limit on role-plays, calling out when one minute is left. Give positive feedback on reps' strengths, and areas for improvement. Build role-plays around your actual products or services so that reps learn while they train. Let your trainees know that role-play is an opportunity to take risks and to ask questions, and that it's all right to make mistakes.

Provide trainees with reference materials (such as price lists). Beforehand, write out the decision-maker's (customer's) role and name, the company name and background, questions and objections the customer may have, and his interest in the product.

Is Role–Play Important?

There are many benefits to role-play. It trains reps on verbal and listening skills, flow-of-call presentation, and products or services. It helps reps to polish their skills, and it relieves their fears. Role-play allows reps to make mistakes and to learn from them, without censure.

Role-play allows reps to think and act like customers. It uncovers gaps in the actual presentations that trainers might have missed, and the technique is inexpensive and easy to work with.

Use role-play to demonstrate how to do specific skills. Probing, for example, is easier to understand in role-play than it is in theory. Role-play can help trainers to identify reps' specific problems, and to devise solutions for them.

Role-play offers numerous benefits as a training tool, but that doesn't mean that it can't be fun. Try some of the following ideas and then use your own creativity to think of even more exercises. Create customized scenarios that relate to the rep's personality. Use managers as "characters" in role-plays, or as actual participants. Exaggerate situations to illustrate how products or services could be used. Have the reps create their own role-plays.

Work celebrities' names into your role-plays. To add a realistic touch, wear costumes, or use props. Try "role-play rotation," an exercise similar to the game of musical chairs we played as children. Explain the background of the role-play to the group. Have everyone sit in a circle, and choose one person to be the customer. Then with the supervisor giving the verbal "stops" and "starts," begin rotating the role-play, with the next rep picking up where the last rep stopped. Build a role-play tape library that includes both serious and humorous sessions.

Quick–Start Training

Give your trainees a head start by developing a "quick-start" program. At one large company, on the first day of training, every new rep is given a "quick start" package. This folder, packed full of information, offers employees a glimpse of the kind of facts they'll learn during training. It's also a useful reference source for new employees. This package might contain some of the following items.

- Highlights of the company's history
- Company business philosophy
- Company organization chart
- Company mission statement
- Methods and activities that trainers will use to teach telemarketing, including a tour of the center, an explanation of presentations, assigned readings, videotapes, audiotapes, role-play, purpose of the center, types of calls, rep job description, basic marketing principles, types of products/services offered by the company, and customer profiles
- List of acronyms used by the company
- Glossary
- Crossword puzzle or quiz to test the reps' knowledge after reading the package

During training sessions, highlight the benefits of working for your company. Give complete information on pay scales, bonuses, contests, personal benefits, and your promotion policy. This is also the time to establish rules, and to discuss the daily reality of the workplace. What is a typical work shift like? Tell the good, as well as the bad. Talk about dress codes, and the proper conduct expected on the job.

Common Training Mistakes

One common training mistake is lack of adequate practice. Give your reps plenty of time to hone their skills by role-playing with you and with the other students, or by tape-recording their practice sessions. Another mistake is lack of model behavior. Present model behavior through your own role-play of a call, through the example of one of your top reps, or in the form of a printed model script. Yet another mistake is lack of specificity. To improve a rep's calls, work on only one skill at a time (closing a sale, e.g.). Never attempt to improve the entire call, because a call may contain many different skills.

Add Variety to Training

Add variety to training through the use of various aids and activities, such as audiotapes, films, slides, posters, games, and books. Attend industry seminars and conferences to discover how other companies train. Talk with other trainers to gain fresh ideas. Subscribe to magazines and newsletters about training and telemarketing. Regularly review and revise your in-house training program.

Ongoing Training

Training never really ends. The manager must create training that's innovative, yet effective. Show reps how to become responsible for their own (and others') training to make the process much easier. When reps feel that they have input and control over the direction of their learning, they'll be more willing to accept training. Ask your employees for ideas and for new methods of training. Teach them to share both good and bad experiences; everyone learns from both successes and failures. Encourage reps to present the problems they've encountered and the solutions they've devised. Share training ideas through the company newsletter.

Keep your reps informed. Has a customer ever called your center to ask about a new product, only to find that your reps knew nothing about it? Keep your reps informed about all the newest products and services you offer. Give them copies of press releases about any company-wide changes. Supply your group with direct-mail pieces, and copies of print ads. Reps can use this material as reference sources when they're on the phone with customers. Such handouts increase the reps' confidence, and make them better informed.

If you implement new rules, discuss them first with your team. Include some of their suggestions to promote their acceptance. Don't let a memo concerning an upcoming change come from above without warning your reps first.

Develop a set of lessons for your in-house training program. Each lesson should concentrate on an individual skill. This approach makes it easier to design refresher courses and to add to and update your training program. Always look for new training tools, such as current newspaper or magazine articles, new training exercises, or videotapes. Create a "telemarketing library" for your trainers and reps, so that they can keep abreast of the latest techniques and events. Don't forget to update all your training materials, including student binders, handouts, scripts, and price lists.

During the first week of rep training, bring in a panel of experienced reps to describe to new hires what to expect on a typical day. This panel can also discuss how to handle problems, deal with angry customers, make sales, and how to deal with rejection.

Have your reps give a brief presentation on some aspect of telemarketing. Other reps may identify more strongly with a fellow employee than with a supervisor.

Train with audiotapes. Before the training session, select some taped calls to illustrate key training points. In class, play a portion of a tape and then stop it. Ask one of your reps to assume the role of the rep on tape, and then to take the call to the next step. Repeat this exercise with a few reps. Let the group judge which rep made the best presentation and why it was effective. Compare the reps' presentations with the taped presentation.

Ask your reps to give an example of poor service (in restaurants or stores, for example). Ask them how the service provider acted. What did they think of the company and the service it provided? Ask the reps what makes good service. What does your company do to promote good service? How can your company improve?

Have experienced reps share their expertise with new reps through a "buddy" system. During the first few weeks on the job, new hires can go to their senior "buddies" for advice and information. This technique will bring the new reps up to speed quickly.

At least once a month, hold a 30-minute "awareness" seminar highlighting different departments in your company. During one such session the accounting department could explain its function; the advertising department might bring its newest print ads; a scriptwriter might describe how he creates a script for a new campaign. Present the same session several times so that all your reps get a chance to attend.

Plan a fair showcasing your company's products and services. Add excitement with hands-on demonstrations, prizes, small giveaways, brochures, and refreshments.

Create advanced-training lessons to challenge and maintain your seasoned reps' skills. Lessons might focus on: listening skills, stress management, use of analytical skills, cross-training, and dealing with customer complaints.

The benefits of cross-training to you and your reps are many. Cross-training builds a better understanding of other departments, and fosters teamwork. Interest levels remain high while boredom decreases. Employee turnover also declines when tasks are varied. Cross-training can also prepare reps for promotion.

Cross-training gives reps an idea of what happens to an order after they take it. Reps can learn about your products from observing the assembly process in the factory, or by discussing the technical aspects of products and services with the managers. The knowledge gained can increase reps' confidence when they sell.

If your center handles incoming and outgoing calls, training your reps to do both enables them to rotate jobs. Achieve more job variety by teaching employees clerical functions, as well as their primary functions.

At one large airline's direct-marketing center, the supervisors' desks are positioned in the middle of the floor, and their reps' work stations are placed around them. The supervisors are always available to answer unusual questions, make suggestions, and to cheer their people on. The positive impact is extraordinary.

Offbeat Training

Compile a list of reps who are experts in the various steps of a call (building rapport, closing a sale, handling objections). Trainees can call upon these experts when they encounter specific problems. Managers can refer to the list when they develop new projects, write scripts, or try to fix an ailing campaign.

Encourage reps to identify an area for improvement or to implement a new process in the center. Empower the reps to "own" the project from initiation to completion.

Develop a self-instruction program when you only have a couple of new reps to train and time is short, or when reps need a refresher course. Program components might include the following.

Basic training manual The manual must address all of the subjects to be learned during training, and it must clearly explain the key areas of knowledge and skills. Audiotapes of examples of both good and poor calls (between reps and customers) should be incorporated into the program.

Include written exercises, borrowed from other programs, to reinforce new principles and to provide practice in applying new skills. Manuals can be prepared inexpensively.

During training, refer students to supervisors for more help. Have trainees listen to live calls and participate in role-plays. Introduce role-play by giving background information on the procedures and techniques to be used. Training manuals can be easily updated by printing price information and product descriptions on separate sheets and in inexpensive binders. In fact, if you're just starting a small center, begin your self-instruction program simply with single sheets of training material, and then build from there. After your center is established, build a more sophisticated program.

Audiocassettes Create or purchase tapes that provide examples of various customer-contact scenarios. These cassettes should reinforce the approach reps must use to sell with their voices and words. After listening to the tapes, students should do role-plays with their supervisors.

Student workbook This book should contain the written exercises, samples of forms actually used in the center (for reps to practise with), evaluation forms for critiquing calls, and background information for role-play. Save time and money by using separate sheets placed in a folder with pockets.

Instructor's guide This guide will explain the purpose of the training program, the materials needed, the learning time required, and it will list the teacher's responsibilities. Guidance should be given for practice sessions. Methods should be specified for determining when trainees are ready to work on the phones.

Reference guide This guide should be used during training and on the job. It should contain critical information about products and services.

Training "On the Run"

Look for training opportunities; there are hundreds around you. Tap your creativity to set the stage for a positive training environment. Like fast food eaten "on the run," offer fast training "to go."

At the beginning of a shift, pose a question to your reps, on paper or displayed on the reps' computer terminals, about a selling skill, a product or service, listening skills, or on building rapport. Broadcast the answer near the end of the shift.

Display a new product in the lounge, or pass around brochures about services you offer. Encourage reps to share their ideas about organizing customer information, recording data, or managing their filing systems. Publish these ideas in your house newsletter. Display catchy, educational posters throughout the center. Change the posters frequently.

Pass around one-page fact sheets to keep important product information fresh in the reps' minds. Show short (ten- to fifteen-minute) informational videos to the group. Give your reps for their own use the products or services you sell to help them believe in what they sell. Of course, you might not be able to afford to do this with expensive items. Enthusiasm and a positive attitude are both "contagious." Use motivational videos, posters, pep talks, and supervisors' upbeat attitudes to help reps visualize success. Adapt television game-show formats to review telemarketing concepts.

When calls taper off, reps can use their computer terminals to display five- to ten-minute training lessons. Use this technique to update your reps' training. Encourage your supervisors to use the first ten minutes of each shift to meet with their groups to disseminate new information, or changes in a campaign. Use customized training cards. On the left side of an index card, list product features. On the right side, list corresponding benefits. Small cards can remind trainees to smile when answering the phone, or to say "thank you" at the end of a call. New reps can forget the "little things" that experienced employees take for granted.

Tailor the Rep to the Position

It's important to fit the right rep to the right telemarketing position. You can't always expect reps to handle all types of calls. A new rep may only be ready for simple order-taking, while a seasoned rep can handle complex products and services, or probing-type calls. You'll achieve good results by assigning high-potential customers to the reps best suited to "prospecting," or to closing sales. This tactic can also be an incentive for new reps—they can always work their way up to handling more complex calls.

To discover your reps' expertise, have them write down the answers to these questions:

"With which products do you feel knowledgeable enough to teach others?"
"How do you overcome objections?"
"What are your strongest selling skills?"
"How do you stay motivated?"
"What are your best tactics for calming an angry customer?"

Analyze the answers. Supplement the results with what you already know about your employees' skills. Place the reps in the campaigns for which they're best suited.

Characteristics of a Successful Rep

A rep's goal is not to counter every objection. His goal is to complete the sale. Reps who know the competition can anticipate comparisons and formulate responses. Top reps speak to customers using the customers' language. They answer objections by citing the benefits to the customer. They don't take objections personally—they respond in an agreeable manner. These reps listen to the customer's side of the conversation. Listening helps them determine that the customer has made a decision to buy. These reps close the sale, rather than talking themselves *out* of a sale.

Pick Winners

Michael J. Marx, President of Selection Sciences, Inc., has conducted studies on the personalities of top reps. He's developed a list of knowledge, skills, and abilities to identify and categorize various types of reps. To identify winners, Marx suggests that you ask your reps to arrange the items listed below in the order that's most needed to successfully sell your products. The items high on your best reps' list are the items you want in the next reps you hire. Compare your top and bottom reps.

1. self-confidence
2. financial rewards
3. job variety
4. praise from supervisor
5. personal commitment
6. integrity
7. extroversion
8. attention to detail
9. ability to learn quickly
10. ability to close a sale
11. flexibility
12. ability to be liked
13. concentration
14. ability to follow procedures
15. tolerance for stress
16. rapport-building
17. emotional stability
18. team playing
19. high energy
20. ability to handle rejection
21. ability to keep organized
22. speaking skills
23. internal motivation
24. competitiveness
25. value on time

Compensation Plans

Put your compensation plan in writing. Make it simple, and use illustrations. Portray potential earnings at different sales levels. The more control the rep has over his sales, the more varied the compensation plan can be. Explain when payments will be paid, and on what basis. Note any limits on earnings. Supervisors should review the compensation plan with new employees. Of the many compensation plans available, straight salary is the most unattractive, because it doesn't distinguish between good and poor performance, nor does it stimulate improvement.

Be Sensitive to Change

As a manager, be sensitive to change, and the impact it has on reps. For example, the transition from a manual to a mechanized environment can terrorize a telemarketing center. Discuss changes with your employees before they happen. Do this in a positive manner, emphasizing the benefits that they'll derive from the change. Obtain and include their opinions as part of the change. Demonstrate how easy the change will be. A complex change may need to be introduced in steps, with the basics presented first.

3
MONITORING

Many reps dislike the very idea of monitoring, tensing up if they think their supervisor is "on the line" during a customer call. Reps wish this intrusive eavesdropping would just magically disappear. Supervisors may view the procedure as dully routine. They dutifully do their week's quota of calls, fill out the forms and counsel. The next week rolls around, and the whole process begins again.

Pending legislation threatens to restrict monitoring practices in many localities. What can be done about monitoring?

Develop new tactics that are strong enough to negate monitoring's drawbacks. Create a process that's a *plus* to all participants, instead of a necessary chore. Remove your reps' fear of monitoring, and let them see it as an opportunity to develop their telephone skills. Challenge your supervisors to try new methods. Take risks and, if necessary, turn the art of monitoring upside down to make it work for your center. By developing a new attitude, monitoring can become a challenge that you can learn to enjoy.

Don't feel helpless in the face of current and upcoming legislation. Carry on your business ethically, within the confines of those laws. By practising responsible telemarketing, you may prevent further legal restrictions aimed at the telemarketing industry.

Benefits of Monitoring

Monitoring offers three benefits: 1. Quality assurance. You can ensure that the calls represent your firm's quality and integrity. With each call, the rep is the "company spokesperson." Regular monitoring will ensure that each call is of the best quality. 2. Coaching and development of reps. The best method for helping reps improve is to monitor their calls and then to provide immediate feedback. 3. Customer satisfaction. Customers get accurate information, courtesy, and respect. Productivity rises, and errors decrease.

Evaluating Current Reps

One purpose of monitoring is to evaluate your current reps' performance. Are they doing their jobs? Are they relating well to customers? Are they properly positioning your products or services? Are they generating sales?

You can increase the benefits of monitoring by immediately coaching reps about what you hear during monitoring sessions. A successful telemarketing company believes in coaching between calls. Since their reps continually receive input, morale is high, and the reps are motivated, as well. If this tactic doesn't suit your center, do your coaching one-on-one, promptly after you've finished the monitoring session for that period.

Training New Reps

Coaching, rather than teaching, is important when you train new reps. When you provide feedback to a new rep immediately after a call, the rep is more apt to remember the point. To give feedback, draw on your personal reactions to a call. How did you (as a manager) feel about that last call? Did you enjoy listening to it?

You might start a typical feedback session with a question directed to the rep, such as, "How was that call for you?" Keep the rep's attention by making only one point at a time. Tell the rep what worked and what didn't.

If your monitoring sessions reveal that a rep is still doing poorly, despite coaching, take the rep off the phone and give him or her intensive refresher training, troubleshooting for weaknesses. You don't want to jeopardize quality sales and customer satisfaction with poor-quality calls.

Satisfy the Customer

Meeting the customers' needs is always most important, and ongoing monitoring will help you do that. Differentiate your company from your competitors by striving for excellent customer service 100% of the time. That extra touch—a friendly voice, a value-added service that gives the customer more than he expected—differentiates your firm from another.

At times you may be conducting a campaign for an outside company, on contract, or your "client" may be another department in your own company.

An important element in the success of a telemarketing program is the client's input and participation in the campaign, from script development, to formatting reports, and to training. The client is the expert in his business. It's only natural to have him participate in all phases of your program.

Once you're ready for the campaign, encourage the client to attend the campaign kickoff—to monitor calls, to walk through the center, and to meet with the reps. The client can learn much from the reps who have talked with his customers about prices and products. This approach is also a great morale booster for your reps.

Who Should Monitor?

Managers, supervisors, and those employees whose sole responsibility it is to monitor calls are the people you usually find in the monitoring rooms of many telemarketing centers. Other company employees might also benefit from listening to rep/customer dialogue. Your trainers should regularly monitor to make sure campaign strategy is understood and followed—not only at the beginning of the campaign, but throughout the promotion, as well. Their participation can provide them with ways to improve training lessons.

Those employees who might also benefit include: those from the advertising, systems, billing, customer service, scriptwriting, and order processing/fulfillment departments. By monitoring, your colleagues get crucial customer feedback that will be of benefit to them when they go back to their daily tasks, or when they plan future campaigns. It won't hurt to invite upper-level management. The vice president of marketing should be aware of what his or her customer thinks of the company's product or service. Many times, executives are too far removed from where the real marketing takes place. Customer feedback can help them to develop realistic strategies.

It's also beneficial to include a rep in each monitoring session. Listening to the "live" calls of his fellow reps, and participating in the post-call critiques, helps the rep to improve his own calls. Because reps are on the "front lines," they can also provide insight to discussions about monitoring. Reps can sometimes be more receptive to a peer's suggestions about how to improve calls, rather than hearing criticism from a supervisor.

Other Ways to Bring Reps into the Monitoring Process

Try innovative ideas with your group to keep the process fresh for everybody and to promote team spirit. If a specific problem keeps recurring, have reps put together a "solutions" package and present it to the members of the monitoring team.

At the end of a campaign, ask reps who've monitored to make a presentation of what did or didn't work during the campaign. This could be a real eye-opener. Feature a "techniques that worked for me" column in your company's newsletter.

Quality-Monitoring Workshops

There are many different ways to handle monitoring. It's a challenge not only for reps but for supervisors, too. How can employees have a better attitude towards monitoring? An approach that one company uses is a "quality-monitoring workshop." This workshop was the company's answer to its reps' suggestions about how to revise and improve the monitoring forms. Each workshop was attended by four volunteer reps, a group leader, and a supervisor, with each member having equal voting power. Managers actually went out of their way to recruit the most vocal critics of the monitoring process. There were six sets of workshops, meeting over a four- to five-month span, with five to six half-day sessions in each workshop. The participants' responsibilities included monitoring the calls, evaluating and scoring the calls using existing criteria, revising the monitoring form, testing, and coming to a group consensus. The benefits of the workshops were many. The revised forms and the monitoring itself gained higher levels of acceptance from the reps. Reps saw how difficult it is to evaluate a three-minute call right on the spot. Reps began to understand the importance of "probing" during a call. There was an increased sense of participation in the group. Reps realized the difficulty of scoring (checking off correct/incorrect parts of the call).

Monitoring at the GE Answer Center

Here's another example of a large telemarketing center that makes more of monitoring. At this company, monitoring is viewed by management to be vital; without it they wouldn't be successful. Eighty percent of monitoring is designed to develop the employee; 20% is designed to measure the employee. This emphasis on development takes on a positive flavor, thus decreasing reps' fears. Full-time supervisors are solely responsible for monitoring and coaching.

Powell Taylor, GE Answer Center manager, says that his reps readily accept monitoring. He says, "If you don't monitor people, you'll never know how to develop them, to help them grow and help the business. It's critical for both." When monitoring shows that a rep isn't doing well, more training is the usual remedy.

Name Your Monitoring Program

Monitoring has always had a bad reputation. The word monitoring has the sinister meaning of "being watched." Give a different and more positive name to your own program. Hold a contest and let your reps come up with their own name for the program. Other suggestions for names include: coaching, teaming, service-observing, positive monitoring, auditing, quality checks, customer contacts, and call coaching.

Make Monitoring Part of the Job

Discuss monitoring procedures during your first interview with a prospect. Describe it as just another part of the job. If a prospect does object to on-the-job monitoring during this interview, you'll have found out before you invested in expensive training.

Have each new rep sign a contract or agreement stating that he understands that his calls will be monitored as part of ongoing training and continued employment. See the sample monitoring agreement on page 61. Check and keep abreast of federal, state, and local laws. If you have a legal department in your company, have it approve this monitoring agreement.

From the earliest stages of training, make monitoring a normal part of your center's routine. Reps should know that they're continually monitored, although they should be unable to detect exactly when monitoring is taking place. Tell them that supervisors listen to reps' calls so that the supervisors can let the reps know what the reps are doing well and to suggest how to increase sales. Always use monitoring in a positive manner, to reward rather than to punish.

Tape-Recording for Quality Control

Tape-recording new reps during monitoring sessions can be more effective than just telling them about their errors. The latter implies a sense of blame. One new

MONITORING AGREEMENT

I understand and agree that _____ center
may monitor and tape any of my telephone conversations made in the
course and scope of my work, for the purpose of training, quality
control, and security. I understand and agree that I will not be
notified in advance when this monitoring or taping is taking place
and that _____ center has the sole
discretion to determine the time, place, and manner of all
monitoring sessions.

rep, after listening to a recording of one of her calls, said with surprised horror, "I said *that?*"

Regular taping also provides an objective basis to evaluate a rep's performance, analyze patterns of success and failure, target specific training towards areas needing improvement, and it demonstrates a rep's growth over time. Taping is also more realistic than role-play. Tape calls on a "staggered" schedule so that you get a true sampling of a rep's average performance.

Taping calls can also help seasoned reps to polish their skills. Frequently, because top reps have such good track records, they can become overconfident, and sloppy in script adherence, or they may forget relationship-building principles. A reprimand on deteriorating call quality will not have the same impact as a recent recording of a poorly handled call. Of course, all coaching should be handled in a "praise and reprimand" manner, and should end on a positive note.

Additional benefits of monitoring

Identify training needs Although you'll usually use monitoring to provide feedback and to coach individual reps, this tool can also help you to identify training needs in your center.

Develop standard communication skills During calls, pay specific attention to the ways in which customers respond to your reps' different behaviors. This will let you know what customers expect. With this insight, identify the communication skills you need to develop as company standards.

Instill responsibility During coaching, encourage reps to accept responsibility for their role in their own top performance. Encourage them to take responsibility for ideas and solutions for areas that need improvement.

Market research Listen carefully to what your customers say; you'll gain valuable insight into what their real needs are. Don't add market research questions to your telemarketing call. Rather, view customers' candid responses as "informal" market research. What's on their minds? What interests or bothers them? Record your customers' comments, and soon you'll see a trend. In one center, customers didn't want to pay an order-processing charge, so the company waived the charge during a special limited-time promotion.

Testing scripts Before a new campaign officially begins, test two different scripts. By monitoring (and carefully listening to customers' reactions) you can determine which script more successfully accomplishes your objectives.

Test specific *portions* of your script to see which version is more effective. Test different rebuttals, second attempts, or closing statements. Monitor the calls to gain quick feedback on which approach works best with a customer.

As you continue to monitor, you may hear the same customer complaints repeatedly. This tells you to take a critical look at your product, service, or campaign, and it also shows the need for *scripted rebuttals* to ensure that your reps won't be at a loss for words when a complaint arises. A scripted rebuttal guarantees accuracy and consistency among your reps, so that a unified company statement is presented.

Monitoring can also help you to evaluate your campaign, even before a stack of sales reports lands on your desk. Is your strategy sound? Are you talking to the right customers? Depending on the answers to these questions, you may need to change your positioning, or even write an entirely new script.

Potential clients When soliciting new business, offer potential clients the chance to participate in one of your monitoring sessions. These sessions can be an excellent marketing tool. Of course, you should obtain your current client's approval beforehand, preferably in writing.

Training tapes Tape examples of good and poor calls (actual or simulated) and play the tapes in your training classes. Ask your reps what made the calls good or poor, and how the poor calls could be improved. Use the tapes to create a training library for new reps.

Building bonds Monitoring can also build bonds between managers and reps. The more involved the manager is with his employees, and the more concerned he is about their skill development, the better the working relationship will be.

Measuring and monitoring productivity are not the same. Productivity can be measured quantitatively, that is, the number of calls placed, the number of sales, and other data. By monitoring a call, you get an idea of actual job performance.

Has the rep properly determined eligibility (*qualified* the prospect)? Given thorough and correct product information? You need to determine the overall quality of the call. Monitoring is your best quality-control tool.

Rules for a Good Monitoring Program

- Keep to a schedule.
- Monitor regularly and consistently.
- Revise your monitoring forms periodically.
- Delete obsolete categories from your forms.
- Be innovative.
- Give awards to the top reps each month, or invite the vice president to monitor with you one day.
- Try different ideas to maintain your own interest, as well as that of your reps.
- Keep up with the latest monitoring techniques.
- Read books and magazines on telemarketing, and confab with other center managers.
- Provide feedback when it's due.
- Give constructive feedback early.
- Keep monitoring positive, fun, and upbeat.
- Award (not more than one minute after the call ends) small prizes for the best calls.

Every call you monitor should include the following steps for success.

- Listen to the call.
- Write down what you hear.
- Correctly evaluate the call.
- Complete the monitoring form.
- Analyze the call to prepare for feedback.
- Give immediate feedback to the rep.

Plan Your Weekly Monitoring Schedule

Consider the following when you plan your weekly monitoring schedule. Which campaign will you monitor? Which employees will you monitor? Make sure you check beforehand the days and hours they'll be working. Note when their breaks are. Which skill will you focus on? Bridging to another product? Closing the sale? Plan to monitor about one hour a day, allow for three to four calls and immediate feedback to the reps.

Depending upon your telemarketing application, estimate that you'll be monitoring about ten calls per rep each month. If a rep is having a bad day, it would be unfair to monitor all ten of his calls in one day. Monitor about three calls at one sitting. Using this formula, you'll be monitoring each rep about three times in one month. The proper approach depends upon the needs of your center. These needs may be affected by the type of application, campaign, number of reps and supervisors, training, scripts, product or service promoted, and the size of the center.

When scheduling monitoring during the workday, schedule ample time for feedback, too. Your reps depend upon your feedback for guidance. Don't forget to allow time for interruptions when you plan your schedule, or you may be doing nothing but monitoring for the last one to two weeks of the month.

Consider what the best days of the week, and the best times of the day, are for monitoring. Don't monitor when only a trickle of calls is coming in, or when few customers can be reached through outbound calls. Ask yourself which reps in your group have the most developmental needs. What are those needs?

What specific negative trends have been brought to your attention by other staff members or by client observations? What trends have you been seeing?

Monitoring Forms

Monitoring forms should be customized to your particular campaign, and they should reflect the necessary components of a good call, as well as the campaign's objectives. Start with sample monitoring forms as shown on pages 65–67. Personalize the form until it fits your needs. Forms can range from a simple, one-page checklist to a two-page, detailed breakdown of a call. If you delegate your monitoring to others, the longer form may be best for you. Your monitoring form should rate verbal skills, listening skills, relationship-building skills, courtesy, sales presentation, and closing techniques.

At the beginning of a new campaign, test a few forms before you find the one that best meets your needs. Once your team becomes more experienced with monitoring, checking for call quality becomes easier. At that point, careful listening enables you to get the "feel" of a call, knowing if that call projects your company image and goals.

Monitoring forms can help you in many ways. They can be an effective tool for managers, because a standard form ensures consistent quality. The forms provide reps with a blueprint for handling calls effectively. Reps can use the forms for self-help and to improve their calls. The forms allow you to observe employees' performance over a period of time. Forms are an excellent resource when conducting performance reviews or annual reviews with your reps.

Develop a monitoring form for each different type of telemarketing call, because each call has its own objectives, and its own sequence of steps, techniques, and procedures that reps must follow in order to achieve the purpose of the call. Forms should also reflect the differences between inbound and outbound calls.

Rate the quality of calls by assigning points.

0 = Unsatisfactory
1 = Needs Improvement
3 = Meets Required Standards (a good call)
5 = Achieves Excellence

Vary your methods of monitoring to give you a better idea of your reps' performance and make monitoring more interesting. Some examples follow.

MONITORING REVIEW

Partner: _____   Coach: _____

Date: _____ Time: _____ AM PM   Score: _____ (100%)

OPENING THE CALL (5 Points)	_____	Greeted Customer
	_____	Identified Company
	_____	Identified Self
	_____	Offered Assistance
	_____	Courteous Manner

GATHERING INFORMATION

(5 Points)
- _____ Verified Phone Number
- _____ Verified Customer Name/Spelling
- _____ Verified Key Number/Customer Number
- _____ Made Credit-Card Inquiry/Verified
- _____ Verified Address/Spelling

BUSINESSLIKE CONDUCT (10 Points)
- _____ Displayed Positive Attitude
- _____ Maintained Control of Call
- _____ Paid Attention to Customer
- _____ Exhibited Effective Oral Communication Skills
- _____ Demonstrated Concern (Acknowledgment Statement)

USE OF VOICE (10 Points)
- _____ Tone (Energetic & Enthusiastic)
- _____ Volume and Pitch
- _____ Word Choice/Grammar
- _____ Pace
- _____ Articulation/Pronunciation

LISTENING & RESPONDING (15 Points)
- _____ Provided Accurate Answers
- _____ Verified Product and Cost
- _____ Retained Information
- _____ Used Customer's Name
- _____ Responded to Customer's Needs

PROBING / CROSS-SELLING (30 Points)
- _____ Used Open/Closed Probes to Make an Offer (3)
- _____ Used Open Probes to Explore Additional Needs and Opportunities without Presenting a Product (10)
- _____ Focused On & Presented Relevant Benefits (5)
- _____ Varied Product Choices (5)
- _____ Handled Resistance & Objections Well (2)
- _____ Overcame Resistance & Objections Well (5)

PRODUCT KNOWLEDGE (20 Points)
- _____ Displayed Extensive Product Knowledge
- _____ Was Familiar with Location of Products in Catalog
- _____ Demonstrated Self-Confidence/Credibility
- _____ Took Initiative to Answer Product Questions

CLOSING THE CALL (5 Points)
- _____ Provided Order Number
- _____ Provided Subtotal & Shipping Cost
- _____ Provided Approximate Delivery Date
- _____ Thanked Customer by Name
- _____ Maintained Courteous Manner

COACH'S COMMENTS: PARTNER'S COMMENTS:

MONITORING FORM

	How well it was done	Ways to improve
The opening		
Introduction		
Adhering to the script		
Closing the sale		
Using features and benefits to help make the sale		
Selling the right product to the right customer		
Other general notes on the call		

Monitoring Form

Rep Name _____   Date _____

Strengths:

_____ Listening Skills
_____ Businesslike Conduct
_____ Enthusiasm
_____ Pacing
_____ Politeness
_____ Diction
_____ Followed script
_____ Verified Name/Address
_____ Sounded Conversational

_____ Obtained correct
            information
_____ Correctly handled
            objections
_____ Clearly described
            offer
_____ Expressed benefits

_____ Branded Call

Comments: _____

_____

_____

Future Goals: _____

_____

_____

Reviewed by: _____

Remote monitoring allows "natural" observation of calls, since reps don't know you're listening. The reps will be relaxed during the call.

Parallel (side-by-side) monitoring can help you evaluate many aspects of a call. How do reps use their computer terminals? How well do they use resources such as handbooks? Are reps coding transactions correctly? If a problem arises, you're there to give immediate feedback. This type of monitoring is also good to use with new reps because you can maintain good eye contact. Reps can indicate when they're in trouble, and you can jot down notes to help them, or point to answers in the reference guide.

Use these techniques for parallel monitoring. Before you sit down next to the rep, let him know that you'll be listening to some calls, and that you'd like to sit down with him. Be conscious of your proximity and body language. Don't sit too close to the employee. Assume a relaxed posture. Establish a nonthreatening atmosphere. Smile. Agree on a way to put the customer on hold. Hold up an index card saying, "Hold," or gesture with a "Time-Out" signal. Avoid interrupting the call at all costs. However, if *not* interrupting the call negatively affects the customer, then interrupt.

Be careful of your nonverbal behavior, and avoid negative facial expressions. Don't talk to others while monitoring, and avoid unnecessary movement. The rep might think you're restless. Don't distract the rep. Observe only three calls at a time. Most of all, don't forget to give immediate feedback in private.

You can gather valuable information through passive monitoring. Walk through the center and listen to what's being said. What are your reps saying to customers? Do they sound polite? Are the reps talking to each other, creating background noise? What does the center's environment tell you? Passive monitoring can help you correct sloppy work habits as they occur. You can help keep morale high with words of encouragement.

Self-monitoring is another approach. With this method, the rep tapes his best call of the day (or week) and then gives it to his supervisor at the end of an agreed-upon time. The rep reviews his own calls and identifies areas for improvement. This approach enhances the rep's listening skills. During this process, a rep usually tapes a call, and then erases it when he completes and tapes a better call.

Here are some developmental activities to use to help your reps improve their telephone skills. Depending upon the situation and the person involved, some activities may be more effective than others. Try these ideas, change them if you need to, using the ones that best fit your center. Use the "stop-watch" technique if your rep has a difficult time controlling the call. Time how long the rep talks and compare it to how long the customer talks.

In "reverse role-play," you act out the role of the rep, and the rep acts as the customer. Go through some simulated calls together, emphasizing the rep's weak areas. Don't forget to praise before you correct. Ask the rep to keep a tally sheet of specific activities or skills to help bring these items to the rep's conscious level. For example, ask the rep to track the number of times he used a "second attempt" during his calling shift.

Do a "regular" role-play. You play the customer. Tape the role-play. Ask the rep how he thinks the call went, and then play back the tape. This is a good activity if a rep can't recognize his own weaknesses.

Practise "peer monitoring." The rep listens to *you* making "live" calls, or he sits with a rep who's good at the skill you want the trainee to learn. Take turns monitoring. Sit down with a rep and alternate "live" calls. The supervisor monitors the rep, and then the rep monitors the supervisor. One-on-one coaching builds team spirit.

Try group monitoring. Gather a small group of reps. Play a tape of one rep's call, and let him critique it first, noting both the positive points and the weak areas. Everybody, in turn, makes comments on the positive parts of the call. Group members then suggest areas for improvement. Taping "live" calls brings telemarketing theory to life.

Do "masked" monitoring by taping a variety of calls in your center. Play the taped calls in training sessions, and let the reps evaluate the calls. Don't reveal the identity of the reps you taped. Reps will feel free to critique the calls, since the taped rep's identity is unknown.

Hold a "my best call" contest. This is similar to self-monitoring. Instruct reps to tape themselves (doing some self-monitoring first), and then to turn in what they think is their "best call ever." The rep will feel comfortable hearing himself on tape, and there's the added excitement of a contest. Depending upon the size of your center, the contest can last anywhere from four to six weeks. Choose winners in each group, each campaign, and finally the best call of the center. Having more than one winner promotes team spirit. This contest is a winner for you, too—you'll have an excellent set of training tapes.

Give reps monitoring forms so that they understand the skills they should strive to perfect, and so that they learn to critique constructively. Teach them to look for the positives first, and then to pinpoint areas for improvement.

Coaching can be as easy as leaving a note on a rep's computer terminal or desk reminding him of something you want him to do. A note might read, "Remember to say, 'Thank you for using our company.' " Keep the notes positive and light.

Giving feedback to employees is difficult. Maybe that's why it's easy to monitor and easier to put off feedback for a day, or a week. View monitoring as just another part of your daily work life; a part that fosters continuous improvement in meeting customers' expectations. Here are some ideas you may want to use during feedback sessions. When you listen to calls, focus on audible or observable behavior, rather than on a personality trait. First ask the rep to identify what changes are needed. This tactic tends to reinforce good behavior. Don't merely tell him what's wrong.

Emphasize the desired behavior, instead of the behavior you want to correct. All feedback should be one-on-one, done in a private area. Offer a model of the proper way to perform a skill. Encourage change (let's say to improve a rep's opening) by letting the rep write a model opening that will create interest, instead of just giving him one to use.

Effective feedback is specific. Don't say, "You rushed that call." Say instead,

"You could have probed more for the sale." Be specific when you praise, too. Avoid dictating change to your reps. Involve the reps by encouraging them to create their own ideas for improvement. Let employees be the ones who create the steps to take and dates to meet for achieving change. Work with your reps to negotiate reasonable goals.

Taping calls offers many benefits. A rep will be open to change when he hears himself on tape. Taping makes it easy to critique the call, since the manager can stop the tape at the point where change is needed.

Don't use the word "but." Use "and" or "the next time." Keep feedback sessions short and positive. In fact, always end the sessions positively. Refrain from saying, "I've been monitoring your calls." Say instead, "I've been listening to some of your calls." Obtain direct quotes from a call. This enables you to be very specific and you'll be able to make your point clearly.

Avoid useless feedback. Telling a rep that he has to improve his attitude doesn't offer constructive information. Instead, encourage him to smile more during the call, or to imagine what the customer looks like.

Score the employee in every category of the call. Base the score upon how well he performed in each step of the sales process, or in each step of the customer-service call. Give extra points if the rep went beyond the usual requirements of a call (cross-selling when it wasn't required, for example). The first few words of feedback determine how the rep accepts the critique. After correcting the rep, don't carry a grudge. Both of you should part on friendly terms.

Know what *you* want from your reps during a call. After the session, document all feedback and set a follow-up date in your planner for assessing the rep's improvement.

80%/20% Feedback

A rep should do most of the talking during the feedback session. Supervisors should strive for an 80%/20% dialogue ratio. The rep should be speaking 80% of the time, and the supervisor only 20%. The supervisor's role is only to guide the dialogue. If the supervisor has analyzed three calls during monitoring, he should identify one or two (at most) skills that can be worked on. You might want to improve just one skill at a time.

Monitoring Don'ts

Don't overload your reps by providing too much feedback at once. Effective learning takes place in small steps, not in giant leaps. If more than one or two areas for improvement are given at a time, the rep may forget some of what he's told, and he may become discouraged, as well. Choose the most serious area of concern first, and then counsel the rep. Once he improves, go on to the next improvement area.

Don't forget to praise. If a rep hears only criticism, he will get tense every time he's monitored, or whenever a supervisor walks by.

Don't provide feedback for a call you only listened to partially. If you only hear part of the call, you won't get the total picture, and you may give the rep incorrect feedback.

Don't provide feedback to the reps days or weeks after you've monitored calls. The rep may not even remember the call. Your impression of the call won't be fresh.

Don't praise your rep, throw in a little criticism, and then heap on some more praise. This usually occurs when a supervisor doesn't feel comfortable criticizing the rep. This sends the wrong message to the rep; he'll think he's doing fine. Be clear about the model behaviors you expect to hear.

Don't monitor irregularly. Reps tend to ignore scripts and proper procedures when they aren't monitored regularly.

Don't ignore your top reps. They need feedback and nurturing, too.

Techniques to Try in Feedback Sessions

Positive reinforcement

Don't talk about everything that occurred during a call. Be specific. Listen for and pick out specific, strongly positive statements made during the call. Tell the rep why the call was positive (from your point of view). Ask the rep why the customer may have liked the call. Encourage the rep to continue this behavior. Positive reinforcement encourages repetition of the behavior.

Teaching

Teach only when the rep doesn't clearly understand how to perform a task. Begin by establishing a supportive environment. Ask the rep, "How do you think your calls went today?" Perhaps a monitoring session revealed that your employee's wrap-up portion of the call was weak. Determine if the rep fully understands the importance of the wrap-up. Your next comment might be, "Let's focus on wrap-up today. Mary, what's the purpose of the wrap-up in the sales process?" If the rep answers correctly, reinforce the correct response. If part of the answer is correct, acknowledge that which is correct, and then provide additional feedback as needed.

If the rep doesn't answer correctly, then she lacks a clear understanding of this step. Your next action is to begin teaching. Ask, "Mary, why do you think it's important to wrap up? How does this step affect the success of the call?" Lead the questions to the point where the employee tells you why the wrap-up is important. Through effective progressive questioning, you'll help the rep arrive at the correct answers. When the rep realizes why the wrap-up is important, work out some developmental activities for her to do so that she can improve her skills. Schedule a follow-up meeting to check her progress.

Corrective feedback

Create a comfortable environment and ask for the rep's feedback on her day's calls. Tell the rep what you'd like to focus on if she doesn't bring up the topic you want to discuss. Ask the employee to describe the correct behavior. If the rep responds correctly, reinforce her correct answer. If you know that she knows how to perform the task, because she's done it in the past (but now may have slipped into a bad habit), begin corrective feedback.

Determine why performance has deteriorated. There can be three possible causes: lack of knowledge, lack of motivation (frequently occurs with seasoned reps), or a change in environment (work schedule, or seating). Try to understand the reason. Mutually agree upon a solution. Have the rep suggest activities that would lead to a solution. Reinforce how the correct behavior will enhance the employee's performance. Ask the rep for a summary statement of the feedback session to test understanding, and to gain her commitment to improve.

Training Check

To check the effectiveness of a rep's training, ask the rep to tell you how to respond to an objection, how to close a call, or how to qualify a customer. If you hear that many of your reps aren't following standard procedures for different parts of a call, this may indicate that the reps weren't adequately trained.

Help Reps Find Solutions

If you want your reps to find ways to improve their calls, ask them, don't tell them. Ask, "What do you think we could do to increase your efficiency?" If a rep has no solutions, make a suggestion and ask him how he feels about it. Suggest some idea that has worked for other reps. Ask, "Do you think that might help you?"

Legal Issues

Taping reps' calls, as well as silent monitoring, both fall into a grey legal area. When you monitor a rep's call, you're also monitoring the customer. To minimize your organization's legal risks, analyze your monitoring procedures with respect to federal, state, and local regulations. Laws vary from state to state. Check any negotiated work rules your company may have. Include a provision in the rep's employment contract stating that periodic monitoring and taping of calls will be done for training purposes. Have the rep sign the contract. The use of any tapes should be limited to in-house training.

Motivating Monitoring

Monitoring should offer more benefits than just improved call quality. To add some fun, maintain an incentive closet stocked with awards for good monitoring: mugs imprinted with your company logo, umbrellas, key chains, notepads, restaurant gift certificates, movie passes, canvas tote bags, watches, pens, T-shirts, and luggage tags. Print award certificates for reps to display in their work stations.

Give an award to a rep immediately after an outstanding call. This creates an element of surprise, boosts morale, and makes monitoring palatable for the reps.

Award prizes to your supervisors (and those who monitor on a regular basis) for the most calls monitored, best call of the week, or for the most sales monitored. This may make the task less onerous for them.

Award points to reps for meeting certain objectives during a call, such as using the second attempt, or skillfully handling objections.

Reps can accumulate points for cash awards, or they can choose from an assortment of gifts from a specially designed company catalog. Here are some suggestions for awarding points for different parts of the call:

Award five points each for each category: introduction, listening skills, accuracy, recapping product information, closing the call, qualifying the prospect, product/service presentation, and answering objections.

Outside Monitoring

Some telemarketing centers use the services of a third party to measure their customers' satisfaction with telemarketing calls. The third-party vendor will usually call a sampling of customers sometime after the original telemarketing call was placed. Customers are asked a series of questions to determine if the call was properly handled. Unsolicited comments are also recorded. At the end of a month, the third-party vendor provides the center with an overall rating on customers' satisfaction with the calls. The telemarketing center usually knows if the ratings are acceptable. This practice offers a way to provide consistent, excellent call quality to customers.

Check Call

One way to monitor call quality is to make "check" calls—call your company and pretend to be a customer. You'll be checking for proper greeting, product knowledge, relationship-building, and sales technique, and you might also want to work in some objections to find out how your reps handle them. In fact, you could design a "check" call form to consistently track your objectives. One company tests its own outbound calls by having its supervisor pose as the employee of a fictitious company. Their reps call this fictitious company, and the quality of the call is monitored.

Things You Might Forget

Count the number of rings before a rep answers an inbound call. Do you receive many calls from prospects who are trying to reach a different company? Perhaps your 800 number differs by one or two digits from another company's number. Encourage your reps to immediately report things like this.

Track the number of busy signals and disconnects in your outbound calls. You may want to install "predictive dialling" in your center. Track the number of times a caller is put on hold. Check headsets to be sure that they're working properly. Check to see if the rep properly identifies himself. Is the rep "branding" the close of the call with your company name? ("Thank you for using ABC Travel!") Call your center and check for distracting background noise. Can you hear the other reps talking?

4

SCRIPTS

As telemarketing becomes more sophisticated through the use of telecommunications technology and the wide use of marketing tools, so will the art of writing scripts. It's no longer possible to churn out a script in an afternoon. You need to know your customers through the use of "niche" marketing. You may need to create customized scripts, sometimes even different scripts for different zip codes. When your reps pick up the phone, they must consider the different customers they're speaking to. Customer profiles have to be developed. You'll continue to use scripts in one form or another, but the quick pace of society demands that you write concise scripts that contain a high value per word.

Telemarketing centers and reps must educate the customer as part of the sales process. Educated consumers are satisfied customers, who know how to get the best out of their products and services.

Your telemarketing center must maintain ethical operating standards. Customers may feel that their privacy is being invaded by telemarketing and direct mail. To aid them in the sales process, telemarketers must use customer information with discretion. Consumers fear "big brother," and they still view the intangible telephone medium with distrust. You must reduce buyers' risk by offering credible, attractive terms of sale.

Approach each call as if it were a personal visit. One center's reps are trained to dress and speak as if they were speaking to the customer personally. This center thinks of "daily customer visits," rather than "calls."

Why Use a Script?

Opponents of scripts may say that all you have to do is properly train your reps, or give them a few bullet points to guide them, and success will follow.

Several years ago, reps at one telemarketing center used bullet points (similar to a guided script) to sell consumer products. Average talk time increased, with one extreme example of twenty minutes for one call. Consequently, costs went up. Each rep was interpreting the "bullet" points in his own way. Customers were not receiving a consistent sales message, and quality was gone.

On the other hand, another of this company's inbound centers was fully scripted, with an average call duration of from five to six minutes. The company took the current script from the second center and adapted it to the needs and restrictions of the problem center. The reps *loved* the script. They didn't have to ad lib, and the reps said that the script made their jobs easier. In fact, full scripting made work easier for the supervisors, and for the company's clients.

If you plan to introduce full scripting to your center, you must get acceptance from your staff. Have them help write the script. Hold focus groups to discuss various sections of the script: the introduction, the closing, rebuttals.

Hold a script "kickoff." Summarize the steps that were taken to develop the script, and the objectives of full scripting. Make the event festive with refreshments and small giveaways.

Do a trial run of the script with a small group of your reps, but don't use just your best people. Your top reps can make even a poor script sound good. Have a good mix of reps.

Your script should never be static. Rework your script until you produce a simple, concise presentation. Use the feedback from monitoring, from the reps, and from the supervisors. Be open to change.

Promotion money has been budgeted. Your product is ready for the market. Now it's time to write your script. Before you do anything else, start *talking* your script. The very idea may sound a little odd to you, but after all, what's a script but one part of a conversation? Your goal should be a script that doesn't sound "canned."

Write Scripts as a Team

Gather together key players in your organization: management, immediate supervisors, staff scriptwriter, representatives from advertising, billing, customer service, and order processing.

Don't forget the most important member of your team, the rep. Experienced reps have learned a lot about human nature, the art of sales conversation, and how to motivate customers to purchase products and services. They're customer-focused, and they can adapt their communication and sales message to target their customers' needs. One rep can help you gain the cooperation of the other reps when a new script is introduced. Reps can also tell you if your script conveys the proper sales message.

Script-Writing Environment

Create the proper atmosphere for your script-writing sessions. Encourage free association and brainstorming. Don't criticize any ideas, no matter how strange they may seem. Post your strategy and position statements on large sheets of paper. As the ideas start to flow, post them on the wall, too.

Surround your group with tools to awake their senses: the actual product, brochures, prior print ads, and old scripts. Obtain vital information from the marketing manager, and write out the product benefits in detail. Post these benefits on the wall. Note any differences that make your product superior to competitors'. Later, prepare "competitive information screens," listing product attributes and prices.

Before you even begin to write, think of all the variables connected to your script. Consider the complexity of the offer, product, or service. Accuracy and consistency are important, as is quality control.

Decide on the amount of relationship-building you need in the script and the type of script that suits your purpose: verbatim, guided, outline, or call-plan. What are your customers' needs? Agree on the medium for your message: paper, cards, or computer screen. What's your target market? You *must* speak to the right people. Remember, the *list* you use is just as important in telemarketing as it is in direct mail. Determine the length of your call.

Objectives Drive Your Script

Write down the objectives of the call and keep them in front of you at all times. Prioritize your objectives. Make sure your objectives can be quantified and tracked: number of sales, number of leads. Your script should focus on having the customer make the decision *today*. Every sentence and phrase should be directed towards the close.

Benefits of a Script

A script helps reps to plan and control the progress and content of their calls. Scripts guarantee consistency of results and the delivery of a standard message. Scripts are easy to test and train on, they encourage focus, and they carry the promise of success.

Without a script, you risk repetition, omissions, inconsistencies, and poor quality. The shortcomings of many presentations may not be caused by the script itself—a script is just words and ideas on paper. Problems occur when reps are not properly trained to communicate with the customer.

Types of Scripts

The complexity of the sales message determines which type of script is best: verbatim, outline, guided, or call-plan.

Verbatim script

Reps follow the presentation word for word. However, reps don't always use the words in exactly the same way in each call. You must continually work with your reps to maintain the same "flavor" of the call. You also need to allow reps some room for creativity. You can only achieve such a balance through consistent monitoring and coaching.

Verbatim scripts are ideal for consumer calls, survey calls, and simple business-to-business transactions. Using such a script lowers training expenses and promotes high standards of quality.

Outline script

This script combines verbatim dialogue (such as introductory and closing statements) with key questions and their possible responses. These scripts are often used in complex situations where there's a possibility that a call might branch off in several different directions.

Guided script

Also known as "dialogue" or "prompt" scripts. These scripts instruct the reps, telling them what must be accomplished during each part of the call. The introduction, benefit statements, and closing are often scripted. The main portion of the call presents suggested questions, responses, as well as rebuttals for typical objections. This script allows the rep to establish a relationship with the customer, and it trains reps to discuss, rather than to read.

Call-Plan script

This script is used by reps who speak to their customers on an ongoing basis. It's still important to follow a simple call plan so reps can control the call, direct its outcome, and achieve the necessary goals. A call plan usually contains objectives of the call, commitments required of the prospects, key questions to ask, a closing, and the next actions to be taken.

Customer Profile

One tool that will help you to write both consumer and business scripts is the customer profile. The profile provides insight into your customers' attributes. Gear your script to this profile to bring you closer to the customer and to promote a conversational atmosphere.

Before you develop your script, list the characteristics of your typical client: background, general characteristics, purchasing behavior, proven sales approaches, education level, and salary and position.

Target your customers even further. Should these people be called again? Maybe there are some customers who just don't need your product. Eliminate them from your base. You might also discover that you have to sell differently to residents of different geographic regions.

Include these steps in every outbound script.

- Verify the prospect's name.
- Identify yourself and your company.
- Tell the customer why you're calling.
- Ask fact-finding or "test" questions to determine if your prospect has an interest in the offer.
- Qualify, establish need.
- Make the sales presentation.
- Overcome objections and ask for the order.
- Verify customer name, address, credit information.
- Read the order back to the customer.
- Thank the customer for the order.

Inbound scripts should contain all of the basic components of an outbound script, except for the opening, which the caller provides.

Socratic Method

Train your reps to use the technique of persuasion first formulated by Socrates in ancient Athens. His technique was based on getting a "Yes" response. Socrates would ask questions with which his opponent would have to agree. He continued to win these agreements until it was apparent that his opponent was agreeing to a conclusion with which he would have disagreed only a few minutes earlier. Encourage your reps and scriptwriters to employ this handy "Yes" response in future scripts and calls.

Screener

Remind your reps that their first sell is to the "screener." One of the screener's responsibilities is to keep out unsolicited calls to the boss, especially sales calls. In business-to-business scripts, reps should treat the screener as an ally. A screener can facilitate a rep's attempt to communicate his sales message to the decision-maker. A well-developed relationship with the screener establishes an open door for continual sales messages, and cross-selling of products. Such a bond also enhances your company's image.

Ways to get past the screener.

- Be persistent.
- Speak with authority and confidence.
- Ask to speak with "Jim" instead of "Mr. Martin," because his secretary will think that you know him, and she'll put you through.
- Call very early in the morning, or call late in the afternoon, when executives answer their own phones.
- Write several call-back options for your reps if they can't reach the decision-maker on the first try. The reps should use a fresh approach for each call to the same person.
- Avoid revealing the purpose of the call to an unqualified prospect, or the qualified prospect may be opposed to your presentation the next time you call.
- Indicate that you'll call back at a more appropriate time if a decision-maker isn't available.
- Provide the screener with only the information that she asks for.
- Don't reveal your name, company, and the purpose of the call in one sentence. The screener may disqualify you.

Opening the Call

An opening statement needs to answer three questions for your prospects.

- Who are you? Identify your company and yourself.
- Why are you calling? Give a reason for calling, plus a benefit.
- What's in it for them? Get the prospect involved.

Here's a sample opening:

"Hello, Mr. Smith, I'm Mary Jones from the Martin Company. I'm calling this evening with an opportunity for you to save on your heating bills."

Remember these steps in the opening. Verify that you're speaking with the right person. Pronounce your name and the name of your company clearly. Tell why you're calling. Determine if the respondent is a valid prospect, and that he's the decision-maker. Assess your customer's mood. Begin with a short, direct statement or question. This gives the prospect a chance to participate in the conversation and serves as a bridge to the next part of the call—the offer. Ask only those questions that will affect the presentation positively. Create a "hook" to gain the customer's attention. Make the customer feel special.

Questions in Your Script

Asking questions creates interaction, provides focus, and increases interest. Question the customer to solicit facts, feelings, opinions, motives, agreements, and commitments. Customers like to answer questions, especially about themselves. When a customer isn't talking, the probability of making a sale decreases. Be sure that your reps understand how to handle the customers' answers.

Ask good questions
- Use the five Ws: Who? What? Where? When? Why? If needed, add "How?"
- Ask questions that have to be answered using more than just one word.
- Ask questions that require others to draw on their experience.
- Ask questions that make prospects explain their viewpoint.
- Ask questions that will guarantee a positive response regarding your product's features, and lead the prospect to the close.
- Ask questions that will help close the sale early.
- Ask questions that determine a customer's needs, so that you offer him the best product or service.

Types of questions

Open-ended questions help you to qualify the customer, stimulate thought, and encourage continued conversation. An open-ended question can't be answered with a simple "yes" or "no."

Use versatile open-ended questions. "What can I do to help you?" "How do you feel about it?" "Can you explain that further?" "What can we change to make this work better?" "What key results are you looking for?"

Closed questions obtain information from the customer, but prevent further discussion. Turn a closed question into an open-ended question by including one or two of these important words: what, how, or could.

Closed-ended question: "Do you use computers?"

Open-ended question: "To what extent do you use computers?"

Add-on questions should be used when you want a customer to expound on a statement or thought.

Customer: "We keep repairing it over and over."

Rep: "You repaired it many times?"

Instructional statements tell the customer to respond. "Tell me what you're looking for." "Give me the details." "Share with me."

"Pre-answer" questions are designed to be answered "Yes." They're based on accurately guessing the prospect's preferences, attitudes, feelings, and beliefs.

"Most people would like to cut costs on . . ."

If you use this "question," prepare a scripted rebuttal for those few customers who respond negatively.

Alternate-choice questions give the prospect the choice of two answers. The customer closes the sale by his own response. "Which do you prefer, the basic or the enhanced plan?"

Reflective questions ask for confirmation by asking the customer to reflect back on an answer he's just given.

Customer: "I need to keep track of a lot of projects."

Rep: "So what you're saying is that your job requires accurate tracking of projects?"

Customer: "Yes."

Rep: "Well then, Miss Lane, are you interested in our monthly planner?"

When you ask an alternate-choice question, customers usually choose the second option. When customers are given a choice of options, and they're asked to choose one, most forget that there's still always one option left—none of the options mentioned.

Sell to Customer Needs

You must probe to determine your customers' needs and desires. A standard presentation given to all customers won't tell you their individual needs. Scripts must be flexible, so reps can do "needs/benefits" selling. Formulate a question (or set of questions) to obtain responses that let reps know which products they should offer, as well as which features and benefits to stress. More than one question may have to be asked to determine the best product to meet a need. Examples of such questions follow.

"How often do you make long distance calls?"

"What's your monthly phone bill?"

The value of the product will be enhanced by creating a *need* in the customer's mind. Use "word pictures" to do this.

Always let the prospect choose between products, but give only two or three options. More than three options might confuse the customer.

Offer, Features, Benefits

An *offer* tells the prospect what you want him to do—buy your product—and what he'll get if he buys it: the benefits of purchasing the product. After you make an offer, ask the customer for the order. The first offer should build upon and enhance the most significant benefits of the product.

A *feature* is a descriptive fact about a product or service. Features define your product. For example, one *feature* of a camera is automatic focus. Features don't sell a product or service; only benefits do.

Benefits turn prospects into buyers. Benefits, not features, answer the prospect's question "What's in it for me?" If you answer the question, explaining how the feature is useful to the customer, then the feature is a benefit. One benefit of an automatic-focus camera is a perfectly focused picture.

Present the product benefits in order of perceived need. Describe the best benefits of the product, that is, "It'll cost you less," or "You'll get more for your money."

If a customer says that he already buys a similar product, and he asks why he should buy from you, your answer needs to be a convincing and strong benefit. Your response must arouse the prospect's curiosity. For example, "We offer immediate credit."

Positive Approach

Be aware of the negative messages you may be inadvertently sending to customers during your conversations.

Rep: "Should I just send information?"
Customer: "Yes."
Rep: "So you don't really make long-distance telephone calls?"
Customer: "No, I don't."

When you make negative statements, you provide the customer with a quick way to end the call. Purge negative words from your conversations as well as "nonwords" such as "Uh" and "You know?" Whenever possible, use the pronoun "you."

Positive	**Negative**
You'll find that . . .	I think that . . .
You'll be interested to know . . .	I wish to point out that . . .

Qualify Your Customers First

There are many benefits to qualifying customers first. This encourages dialogue between the rep and the customer. It cuts talk time by allowing the rep to immediately determine if the customer is a good candidate for your product. Ultimately, you'll lower your costs.

Opening

As a novel must "hook" the reader in its opening paragraph, so must a telemarketing script in its introduction. You'll have only fifteen seconds to create interest with a remark, question, or an initial benefit statement. During the opening, the customer will decide if he likes you, what he thinks you're doing, and how he's going to deal with you. Get to the point quickly, identify who you are, the firm you represent, and why you're calling.

By obtaining the prospect's permission to speak, you're in a powerful position. Be prepared with a ready response if the prospect declines to speak.

A good greeting identifies you and your company. It determines that you're speaking with the correct prospect. It creates a "hook" to obtain the customer's attention. It justifies the purpose of the call with a short direct statement. It draws the customer into the presentation, and it helps determine the customer's mood.

Opening a Business-Sales Call

When you sell to businesses, you must capture your prospect's attention immediately. What can you say in such short time? A few well-planned openings can keep you and your customer talking.

New-Service opening

"New" and "service" are the key words. All businesses like to keep up with the newest developments. Tell your customers about your newest products, and the benefits they provide.

Bargain opening

Everyone loves a bargain. Use this approach to sell overstocked items. Your rep can make a call and offer discounted items. This moves inventory out, and profits in.

Inactive-Account opening

You may have neglected these accounts in the past. Now you're calling to offer a personal customized contact. "Are you satisfied with your products?" "How can I help?" Show the customer that his opinion and his business are important to you.

Before-Mailing opening

Call before you send out a mailing, so you'll be sure that you're sending the letter to the proper decision-maker in the firm. For example, "Mr. Smith, are you the person who authorizes all equipment purchases in your company?" Then determine "Mr. Smith's" primary product interests. In this way, you'll send out the proper literature.

After-Mailing opening

Once you've mailed, you'll have a good reason to make contact with the customer, and you'll have a common subject to discuss. "Did you receive the mailing? No? Well, let me briefly tell you about it." If she did receive the mailing, then, "What do you think about it? Do you have any questions?"

New-Idea opening

When you call your customer and tell him about an idea you have for his company, this shows that you're thinking of his company in a personal and positive manner. Flattery can be an effective tool, and it's a good relationship-builder.

Value of Objections

Objections form part of the natural sales process. When a customer objects, he's really saying, "Give me more information so that I can make an intelligent buying decision." Benefit from the predictability of objections by turning them into advantages. Create standard, structured rebuttals to objections—they'll become winning selling tools. When you write your script, think of all the objections you expect to encounter, and then prepare the best possible responses for each, including an attempt to close the sale at each response. Write your script so that you respond to the objection (thereby satisfying the customer), but then always return to the main script.

Handling objections

Answer a customer's objection with a "Yes," agreeing with him, and then give him a reason to buy, despite his objection. Acknowledge the objection and then overcome it with facts. Point out a benefit that may interest the customer, and then emphasize it.

After you've delivered your presentation, the customer might say that he'd like to think it over. Ask the customer, "Why?" and then answer his next response with a positive-benefit presentation, and then close the sale. If the prospect doesn't answer your "Why," push on with the sale.

Determine which aspect of the offer led to that "No." Probe for more information. Turn a "soft" "No" ("I don't think I can afford it." "I have to discuss this with my wife.") into a sale by responding with a strong benefit.

Asking for literature can be a polite way not to buy. Win the customer over by saying, "Whatever questions you may have, I can answer them right now."

When you follow up direct mail with outbound calls, and the customer asks to be sent more information, say, "That's why I called you today. What other information do you need to help you make your decision?" Learn to distinguish these stalling tactics from legitimate objections.

Use these suggestions to overcome objections. Cite facts and examples (numbers, statistics, details, dollar amounts). Keep your responses and presentation positive to keep your prospects positive, too. Take a customer's objection, and then rephrase it into a question you can answer with a positive reply. After you answer the customer's objection, try to close the sale immediately. Answer an objection by complimenting the customer, and then move on with your presentation. Regularly review your scripted rebuttals. Eliminate the rebuttals that no longer work; add new and stronger rebuttals for any new objections you may encounter.

Answer a customer's objection with a related question, and then follow his response with a strong benefit statement.

Customer: "I don't make many long distance telephone calls."

Rep: "Would you make more long-distance calls if you could call for less money than you're spending now?"

Customer: "Yes."

Rep: "Well, we have a calling plan that lets you do just that."

If you don't have an answer for a particular objection, respond with one of the strong overall benefits of doing business with your company.

If a customer claims that he's tried your product once before, ask him when, and if he was satisfied with the product. Your response should emphasize the improvements that have been made in your product since he last tried it.

Maintain control of the call and the objections with questions and strong follow-up benefits. Never ask a question unless it affects the presentation in a positive way. See pages 86 and 87 for some ideas for answering objections.

Justifying a High Price

Overcome customers' resistance to high prices by using a few of Richard Bayan's phrases from his book, *Words That Sell.*

- It may cost more, but it's worth more.
- Why pay for another product when for a few dollars more, you could have our product?
- Because you're worth it.
- Isn't it better to spend a little more now, instead of a lot more later?
- You'll be billed in monthly installments of just . . .
- Take a year to pay.
- Your credit is good with us.

ANSWERS TO OBJECTIONS

An objection is a valid concern or problem being expressed by your customer. A logical, succinct response to the customer's concern can reassure, or suggest a new perspective to the customer. After you've responded to the objection, go on to close the sale.

o Think of positive responses for each objection.

o Reposition the objection as a small concern.

1. **It's too expensive.**
   A. There are many alternatives and it's very difficult to price the best product for you until we decide which factors are most important. Let's see what will do the best job for you, and at that point we'll determine cost.

   B. Do you mean "too expensive" compared to the results the product brings? If I can convince you that the program I've recommended will bring you new customers and a return on the investment, would you agree with me?

2. **I'm busy. Let me think it over.**
   A. I know you're busy. If there's any question on your part, let me answer it now; while everything is fresh in both of our minds. Then perhaps we can reach a time-saving solution for you.

   B. Let me know what I can do to help you discuss the program. I'd like to arrange for a return call so that you can become aware of how this program can increase your revenues and reduce your costs.

   C. Yes, I can call back later, but before I do, we've discussed several of your business needs and ways this program can benefit you. How do you feel the solutions we've worked out will help you?

   D. If you're not ready now, I can understand, but as a favor to me, please let me know what it is that makes you undecided. Perhaps I haven't been clear enough.

3. **I don't need such a big order this time.** Okay. Let's review the order and see what should be left out. Obviously your needs have changed. I want to give you the best service I can, so let's review your business situation and prepare an order program to match your needs.

4. **Are you trying to sell me something?** Yes. A way to increase your revenue and to save money and time.

5. **I'll talk to my partner.**
A. I understand, but let me ask you how you feel about the program we've discussed. When will it be convenient to talk to both you and your partner? That way I can provide a program to benefit your business and be sure it's acceptable to both of you.

B. Let's discuss the program you think would be best for the firm and then we can discuss the recommendation with your partner.

6. **I don't want any more services.**
A. I'm pleased that you're satisfied with the results you're getting from your current services. Today, most people want things to be convenient, less expensive and more productive. I believe our program can provide you with even better service than you're currently receiving.

B. People in your line of business tell us there have been many changes in the past year. What new challenges do you have this year? How many customers did you add over the past year? Are they slightly or much different from your past customers in their preferences?

C. With the information boom and new technology, everyone's way of doing business is changing. Since things are affecting your business differently, let's take a minute to see how this program could simplify your business and reduce problems for you.

7. **I do business with only a few firms.** You must consider your vendors to be very reliable. However, changes do occur and you may need to be familiar with an alternative to one of those firms on short notice. It's always wise to have a good backup. Let me ask you a few questions so I can clarify what we can offer you as a backup to your current program.

8. **I have more business than I can handle now.** Great! But we all know that business is never static. There are always peaks and valleys. Let me ask you if you're making the kind of profit on the accounts you expect, or if you might be carrying some marginal ones? Let's discuss future growth and be sure you're getting a good return on your hard work and you're getting the best customers.

9. **Business is terrible.** In that case, the competition is pretty stiff. You probably want to take steps to retain your current customers and add more. Let me ask you a few questions to identify ways to strengthen your business position through our program.

10. **My business is too small for your service.** Even the biggest ones were once your size. They took some risks to be successful. Let's look at how you could improve your business with our help.

11. **I'm moving and don't want too much stock around.** Congratulations on your upcoming move. Business must have changed substantially for you over the last year. When will you be at the new location? I'm sure you'll want to be geared up for your opening with the best program you can have. Let's talk about your new business plans for success.

- It'll save you money in the long run.
- Our rates may be higher, but we'll cut costs by getting the job done faster.
- Isn't it worth paying a little extra?
- Don't you deserve the best?
- You probably thought you couldn't afford it.
- You're paying for quality.
- Allow yourself a little luxury.
- A luxury that's within reach.
- Not as expensive as you think.

Script Variables

Consider all the variables in your script: the complexity of the offer, product, or service, the importance of accuracy, consistency, and quality control, the amount of relationship-building needed in your script. Choose the type of script that suits your purpose—verbatim, guided, outline, or call-plan.

Sometimes little things count. These tips will enhance your call. Talk to customers as individuals. Your voice sells, and it must do the entire job of getting the sale. Use a calm, low, pleasant voice—not loud, not too soft, and not monotonous. Don't mumble. Using the customer's name encourages friendliness, and makes the customer willing to buy from you. Use the titles Mr./Ms./Mrs. unless the customer tells you otherwise.

Don't assume that the customer understands everything you say. Repeat important phrases and major points. Use colorful word pictures and examples to help the customer visualize the benefits of your product. Make the call sound as if it were the most important call you're making today. Say "please," and "thank you."

Summarize to help you stay on track during your conversations with prospects. Summarizing is also a valuable selling technique. When you summarize, briefly highlight the main points of your presentation, and the needs or benefits that were discussed.

"Reflective responses" can be used to show understanding and to elicit more information from the contact. Reflect back (verbally) to the prospect's point of view without disagreeing or arguing. These responses encourage your prospect to continue to speak, and they assure him that you're paying attention.

Power of the Pause

After you close, pause. Most customers will feel uncomfortable with the silence and begin to speak, usually agreeing with the rep. Pause during the call. By using the pause strategically, such as, "And her direct number is . . .?" you wait for the information and assume that you'll get it. You aren't asking for it.

Win the customer with these friendly phrases: "May I?" (Asking permission gives your prospect the feeling of authority.) "You're so right." "That's true."

(These give the customer a pat on the back.) "Please," makes the other person feel good. "Because of your background," implies that the person is knowledgeable. "Do you have a few minutes in your busy day?" suggests that the prospect is busy and important. "I'd like your ideas on this," implies that the customer's ideas are important. "I'd really appreciate it if . . ." indicates that the customer has the power either to grant or to refuse.

Don't underestimate the value of premiums. Include a premium, or incentive, in your presentation to improve response rates by as much as 47%. Premiums should be used to induce the purchase of a product, but it won't be the sole reason to buy. Delay offering the premium until the second attempt to close, or if you're about to lose the sale. Free trial offers and special discounts are usually used in business-to-business marketing, but they can work equally well in consumer marketing.

Closing

Reps should always look for an opportunity to close a sale, especially early in the call. Here are some opportunities to be aware of.

Listen for these closing signals

- Customer changes from a cool and argumentative tone to a more relaxed voice. This change in attitude reflects a willingness to purchase.
- Prospect compares the details of your offer with those of a competitor.
- Customer asks to confirm shipping arrangements or other terms of the sale.
- The prospect asks for your opinion, not for product information. This indicates that he now trusts you enough for you to suggest an appropriate product.

Typical closing techniques

Trial close With this early close, gauge the customer's interest. You can often close the sale at this point.

Assumptive close After providing the prospect with the benefit statements, go to the close, assuming that the customer wants to purchase the product. For example, "I can place your order right now." Be ready for any objections.

Assumptive agreement, tag–line close Make the benefit statement, and put a "hook" on the end to encourage the buyer to say yes. "Sounds easy, doesn't it?" Or, "It's great, isn't it?" Now close.

Alternate choice Ask a question with the assumption that the customer will buy. Present two alternatives, and in each case it means a sale. "Mrs. Smith, would you like plan A or plan B?"

Direct close Ask directly for the order. "Mrs. Jones, can I place your order?" Use this close when the prospect responds positively to a benefits-and-features script.

Since you make yourself vulnerable to a "No" response, this tactic is often used as a last resort. However, a "No" answer gives you an opportunity to uncover any real objections the prospect still has.

Elimination-of-choices close Offer the prospect three choices, taking advantage of his indecision. One choice is clearly unsuitable, the next choice is more suitable, and the last choice is the one you're promoting. Offer these three alternatives, saving the best for last, emphasizing its benefits.

Limited-time close This adds a sense of urgency. For example, "If you enroll today, you can save $5.00 off the order-processing charge."

If the prospect doesn't act on your offer, he may lose out on the special discount. This close works well with prospects who want to procrastinate.

The closes described above are meant only as suggestions. Experience, experimentation, and pilot campaigns will all supply you with many new ideas.

Buying-Signal Tip

Listen for "buying signals." If you continue your presentation after the customer gives a buying signal, you may talk yourself out of a sale.

Keeping Sales Closed

Assure that the prospect will be satisfied by stating that he can call your customer-service department should any questions or problems arise.

Compliment the customer on his choice. This allows him to express his own positive feelings about his purchase. The more he talks, the more comfortable he'll become with his decision.

Invite the customer to purchase more products in the future. Your best prospects are your own current customers.

Buyer's Remorse

Some centers use a "verification script" to call the customer twenty-four hours after the sale to verify his order. This step confirms the customer's commitment and also serves as an excellent customer-service tool. Verified orders *remain* orders. Taking this extra step can be especially valuable if you sell expensive items. Unfortunately, the verification call can provide the customer with one more chance to say "No."

Test Scripts

Script-testing never really ends. Managers should continually analyze and monitor the results of different scripts, just as direct-mail companies do with the letters, brochures, and catalogs they distribute. Begin by identifying the number of sales that individual scripts bring in.

What happens when *one* variable of a script is changed, such as the introduction, second attempt, or the closing? Test two completely different scripts against each other, and then use the winner. You might then test the individual components of your winning script. Monitor other factors, as well, including the selling points to which customers most readily respond, and the areas of the script where the call breaks down. Identify questions and objections not anticipated when the first draft of the script was completed. Monitor the effect revised responses (to objections) have on the overall sales rate.

Five basic steps to script-testing

- Tape-record the first draft of your script. Have your team members critique the script.
- Revise the first draft, and record the revision. This time, use role-play.
- Test your script on a customer, using an *average* rep as a control. Your *top* rep can make even a poor script work.
- Now test on a larger scale. Use 50–100 calls as your test block. Pay attention to the weak areas in your script.
- Rework the weak spots in the script, and then test another block of calls.

You'll have many opportunities to test your script—as you create your script, during role-plays, at the trial rollout, and during the campaign. If this is your control script, continually test it to ensure its effectiveness.

Develop an Easy-Listening Script

After you complete the first draft of your script, count the words and put a check mark above every hundredth word. Now go back through the script and count the total number of syllables in every one hundred words. If you have more than one hundred fifty syllables in any grouping of one hundred words, rewrite and simplify your script.

How to Write ("Talk") a Script

Your first step is to first *talk through* the script. Keep the tone of the script conversational, avoid sales talk and encourage dialogue. Long, grammatically correct sentences quickly reveal that a script is being read. Allow for flexibility and variation; take from the spoken word. Use incomplete sentences and contractions just as we do in our daily conversations. Use mostly short sentences. Talk *with* someone, not *at* someone. Build empathy with the customer. Avoid script monologues. Keep the customer talking. Create your script one portion at a time: introduction, product information, second attempt, sale, and close. Write your script so that the customer responds the way you want him to. Be prepared with scripted rebuttals if he doesn't. Prepare a master script, and then write variations for specific campaign needs. Use short, easily understood words—as many single-syllable words as is practical.

Duration

The duration of the call should be just long enough to get the job done. As you work on your script, time the duration, and make sure that your message is concise and to the point. Be sure that all important information is covered. For complex calls, duration may vary. From four to seven minutes should be the maximum duration of most calls. Time your scripts to help you control costs and rep talk-time.

Win and Hold the Prospect's Attention

Answer the most important question in your customer's mind, "What's in it for me?" Tell the customer how long the conversation will take. Try to establish prior relationship with your customer by identifying any past connection that may have existed between him and your company. Use strong descriptive vocabulary in your opening.

Provide opportunities in your script for the customer to talk and to ask questions. Always use open-ended questions so that the customer can't reply with a simple "Yes" or "No."

Silence can sometimes be a strategy. There isn't anything customers *won't* tell you if you're quiet. Not only will they tell you what excites them, but they'll tell you how to sell to them, too.

Keep the description of your product short and direct. During the "offer," focus on only one product or service at a time to avoid confusion. After the offer, mention the benefits of your product.

"How Are You?"

There seems to be some controversy concerning the use of the question "How are you?" in the script's introduction. What's right for your company? Test a script with and without this wording.

Thirteen power words to use in your scripts

They're taken from Steven R. Isaac's book, *Words for Telemarketing.*

easy	guarantee
new	proven
love	results
money	health
safe	you
save	discovery
free (only if you truly offer something for nothing)	

Use motivating phrases

Will you help me?
I'd like to understand your viewpoint.
It's a problem we can solve together.
Thank you!

I'm proud of your decision.
Congratulations!
Please.
You're very kind.
It's been a real pleasure.
Your opinion means a lot to me.

Fact-finding phrases bring the prospect into the conversation

What's your opinion?
What do you think?
Can you illustrate?
What do you consider . . . ?
How do you feel about . . . ?

What happened then?
Would you explain?
Tell me more.
Why?
When is it best . . . ?

Initiate action with these words

you
your
proven
discovery
save
love
safe

results
easy
money
guarantee
free
new
now

Avoid these irritating phrases

Understand?
Get the point?
See what I mean?
You don't say!

Not really?
Don't you know?
I, me, mine, my
I'll tell you what . . .

"Brand" Your Call

Make sure your reps "brand" all calls at the end of their presentation. AT&T reps say, "Thank you for using AT&T." Since these are the last of your words your customers hear, the name will stick in their minds.

Fact-Finding

Request from a customer only the information required. Taking too long to gather data can make a customer impatient. If you want to do market research, do this with a separate call.

Script-Writing Do's

Think visually.

Encourage dialogue with the customer.

Listen to your reps' script suggestions.

Continue to test and revise your script.

Answer the first question in your customer's mind, "What's in it for me?"

Use short sentences.

Build empathy. (Ask with sincerity, "How are you doing?")

At the end of a call, always confirm the order, or repeat the customer's commitment.

Show concern for the customer first, then position the sale.

Provide pauses in the script.

Use motivating language.

Script all warranties, payments, guarantees, liability, and regulatory information.

Use the four Cs: clear, concise, conversational, convincing.

Simplify.

Verify the customer's name and address twice (both at the beginning and at the end of the call).

Script-Writing Don'ts

Use direct-mail copy language.

Use sales-talk language.

Use long words.

Use words that are difficult to pronounce.

Give the customer a chance to say no.

Use script monologues.

Use negative words.

Confuse the customer by over-explaining your product.

Let the customer hear a chaotic atmosphere with fast-talking reps and loud background noise.

Write long wordy scripts.

Use slang or company acronyms.

Use vague messages.

Repeat yourself or your sales message.

Ask objectionable questions.

5

TELEMARKETING FAILURES

Telemarketing is an ever-evolving discipline, readily responsive to quick changes. This very flexibility can itself be the downfall of campaigns, and can lead to unexpected problems. Telemarketing requires constant attention to detail. Due to telemarketing's complexity, every new campaign carries with it the risk of poor performance. Careful management can lower that risk.

This chapter offers a variety of ideas and techniques to help you troubleshoot for potential problems in your center.

A natural tendency is to back away from a faltering campaign, hoping that the memory of it fades quickly. Face that failure and analyze it. Write a brief report, highlighting the key elements of each campaign (success or failure). This report identifies what you've learned from a campaign, what successful techniques you can apply to future programs, what new tools you can use again, what you can try differently the next time. Once you make a mistake in a campaign, it's a mistake you won't make again. When Thomas Edison was asked how he felt after having failed so many times to create the light bulb, he replied, "I did not fail a thousand times, I learned a thousand ways that would not work."

Telemarketing centers can fail for a variety of reasons. Richard L. Bencin, well-known telemarketing consultant and author, says,

> The potential benefits of telemarketing are enormous, but there have been more failures in telemarketing than successes. This is why it pays you to take the significant time required to do telemarketing right.
>
> It is only through careful conceptualization of the program goals and objectives, and a careful development of the sales plan, that the positive, profitable result desired will be reached. And this is true whether an outside service agency is used or the program is carried out in-house.
>
> It often comes as a disagreeable shock to experienced marketing managers that a telemarketing program must be planned and constructed from the ground up. Past experience can suggest, but it won't define how a telemarketing program should be designed. Not all of the approaches, theories, and testing procedures that work for media advertising and direct mail apply to telemarketing.
>
> Telemarketing is a precise, completely controllable, measurable medium. But just as trash into a computer leads to refuse out, poor planning turns the precision and control inherent in telemarketing into a liability.

If you're aware of possible downfalls, there's less chance that you'll repeat them. Ask yourself these questions when a new campaign begins: Is there full commitment from upper management? How about internal communications?

Are all departments kept fully apprised? Am I duplicating efforts? Does my plan cover all possibilities? Do I have a contingency plan? A plan for the worst that can happen? Have the needs/wants of my marketplace been adequately assessed?

One of the main benefits of telemarketing is quick feedback. Use this feedback to your advantage. Improve a campaign by changing a weak script. Early on, carefully track all numbers to help you determine the outcome of your campaign. Update training if reps are becoming careless with their basic skills. Ongoing monitoring will alert you to this slip. You may have to change the direction of your campaign. Telemarketing's advantage is that you'll be able to react to events as they happen, ensuring your center's success.

As a manager, you have a responsibility to give telemarketing a good name, and to help prevent further restrictive legislation. Create goodwill in your community by conducting tours of your center. Make your center a showcase. Let the public see what a telemarketing center looks like: a colorful, airy, pleasant environment for your employees. Conducting tours gives you an incentive to polish and decorate your center; you may even attract some new employees.

By practising responsible telemarketing, you won't alienate your customers. In the long run, you'll promote good relationships with them. Responsible telemarketing includes limiting the frequency of calls a customer and household receives. Customers don't like to be called twice in one week. Keep track of customers who've been called, not only at one center, but at all the other centers your company operates; you'll avoid future duplication.

In the United States you'll be able to use the Direct Marketing Association's (6 East 43rd St., New York, NY 10017-4646) Telephone Preference Service to purge the names of all prospects who don't want to receive telemarketing calls. If you call new prospects who dislike being contacted by telephone, create your own list of customers not to be called. Perhaps you'll promote your service to them through a direct-mail campaign.

Keep track of the rep's name, identification number, time, and duration of call to help you follow up on customers' subsequent questions or complaints. Set a limit on the minimum amount of time between calls to one customer.

Based on telephone numbers, deduplicate your telephone list. Regularly monitor all reps. Use customer-segmentation to offer customers only those products that they're most likely to purchase.

Tactics to Help Avoid Telemarketing Failures

Keep a record of your telemarketing successes (as well as your failures) and how you managed them. For failures, record what you did, and what you might have done to correct the problem. Write scripts that are tailored both to your reps and to your target market. Keep track of customer complaints, both by frequency and by type. Respond to complaints through calls and letters. Send a small goodwill gift with your letter—a product sample, or a "helpful hints" booklet.

During your busy season, hire reps on a seasonal basis, or place reps "on call," offering them financial incentives. Take telemarketing seriously by providing the proper commitment: time, effort, expertise, and money. Don't try telemarketing "on the side" to make some extra money. This approach won't work.

Regularly time your calls, and compare their duration to your standard talk time. Extra minutes can add up to extra dollars. Retrain and coach your reps, if necessary.

View telemarketing as you view your field-sales efforts—as a revenue generator. Don't think of telemarketing as merely a service center, especially your inbound sales and customer-service centers. All selling, including quality customer service, creates value, and generates revenue and profits.

Gather market information and test-call analysis. Which script gives you the highest close rate? Which offer provides the best response? Target and segment your market. Test groups of customers who get mail against those who don't.

Practise quality control with ongoing monitoring, coaching, and training programs. Analyze what has and what hasn't worked to market your product. Learn all you can about your competitors, so your reps will be ready with the correct rebuttals.

Respect the reps' jobs. Motivate and train them with regularity. Don't accept high turnover. Focus on good hiring practices and a thorough training program. Have reps specialize in specific products and services; they'll sound knowledgeable and confident.

Help reps deal with the intensity of the job. Build team behavior by holding sessions where reps can express their feelings of rejection, and share their successes. Offer reasonable (four- to six-hour) work shifts (with proper training and compensation) to stave off exhaustion and lack of motivation.

Teach your reps good listening skills. Poor listening costs time and money, and it jeopardizes good customer relations. If each rep made just one ten-dollar listening mistake per week in your center, think of the lost revenue. Never underestimate the value of what your reps can teach you.

To maintain a dynamic telemarketing center, create an environment of experimentation and innovation. Create a flexible mind-set in your center to enable your staff to look for and solve problems before they become failures.

The Basics

Most telemarketing failures result from neglecting the basics. Even if you're just trying telemarketing, invest money and management time from the outset. Take the time to develop good scripts and reports. Create and implement a full training program. Assign your best management staff to the project. Hire the talent, if you have to.

But, even before you take the steps mentioned above, make sure you've done your market research. If your campaign and your fulfillment procedures are well planned and implemented, but the needs and wants of your marketplace haven't been fully assessed, the program is likely to fail.

The best ideas don't sell themselves; they take time and money. Always plan for the worst. You'll end up with the *best* if you plan all the details in advance.

Tom Peters, author of *Thriving on Chaos*, sees life in business as a series of trial programs. Peters says businesses must learn to innovate fast. "Try, test, adjust, try again, fail, modify, scrap, start over—this must become the normal pattern." Peters claims that "any new idea is, by definition, disruptive." Therefore, he advocates segmenting or "chunking" the project, thereby enabling you to test bits and pieces of it unobtrusively. Slip some of your partially developed new ideas and materials into an ongoing campaign. In fact, when any new idea surfaces, ask yourself some of Tom Peters' questions.

- Where am I going to test it?
- When am I going to test it?
- Can I test a piece of it sooner?
- Can't I do the first test in less time?
- Can't I "chunk" it more?

Later, the questioning shifts.

- What did I learn from this pilot?
- What have I done with that knowledge?
- Are people from other departments part of it?

A daily survival plan is important. Sometimes it's easy to forget daily "checks" that ensure your program's success. Fitting those "checks" into your day can stave off potential problems. Tracking is a daily routine in telemarketing. Spend some time each day reviewing your daily productivity reports. Compare actual results with projections. Set daily goals. Monitor and coach reps daily. Motivation should be built into the daily life of your center. Quality control should be an integral part of your center.

Although you may have a formal "quality assurance" program in your center, audit various activities periodically. Some things you might spot-check include: completed forms, merchandise packed for shipment, stuffing of direct-mail pieces, a specific customer's account and history, process flow of a particular activity (handling a customer complaint, e.g.), any recent script changes, "trouble logs," and your reps' reference binders.

Monitor Your Center

Monitoring means more than just listening to your reps while they're on the telephone. Establish a company-wide program that monitors all aspects of your operation. It's what you *don't* know that can hurt you. To ensure success, keep track of the following items.

Mailings Is direct mail returned to your company unopened? Request an address correction on each letter you send out.

Business lists Clean up your lists by having the reps call first to verify names, titles, and other vital information.

Direct-response network Are all of your 800 numbers in working order? Do you get a ring but no answer when you call? Are the 800 numbers in the proper "hunt sequence"?

Order entry In one center, after a few weeks into a campaign, it was discovered that orders were not being received at the fulfillment house. It seems that computer tapes containing the orders had remained in the center, and hadn't been forwarded. The fulfillment house assumed the campaign hadn't started yet, so it was unaware of the problem, until a chance phone call revealed the mistake. This situation could have been avoided by implementing just a few quality checks.

Monitoring reps If you don't have the time to regularly monitor your reps, hire an outside company to do silent monitoring, or to make "check" calls into your center. An outside vendor can also make follow-up calls to customers to measure their satisfaction with recent telemarketing calls. A telephone survey can also effectively track customers' satisfaction. If you're having a specific problem, don't rely on chance to hear it during monitoring. Tell your supervisors to phone that "problem" call into your center. Their subsequent interaction with the reps during the "problem" call may tell you how to quickly tackle the problem.

Time line A good time line can be invaluable. If small tasks and responsibilities are overlooked, they can lead to large, costly telemarketing failures. The time line guides your progress and keeps you on schedule.

Assign a date to every function to be completed (script development, staff training, etc.) before your campaign begins. Most important, revise your time line often, as you move ahead or fall behind.

Don't make these mistakes

- Reps not planning their calls. Encourage your reps to plan before each call, and to be ready for objections.
- Focusing on the product instead of the customer and his needs
- Reps talking too much. Have them listen, instead.
- Selling product features and technology. Customers want results and benefits.
- Not developing rapport. Match your selling style to the customer's style.
- Not setting daily, weekly, monthly goals. When you set goals, you try harder.
- Not building your own prospect list and data base
- Not differentiating your product and its advantages
- Ignoring the consumer in the business person
- Not awarding loyalty with special offers or discounts
- Automatically applying consumer techniques and solutions to business-to-business problems

- Not doing proper market analysis and targeting, resulting in a large number of outgoing calls, but few sales
- Neglecting to create profiles of productive and nonproductive prospects

Avoid calling telephone subscribers who have unlisted or unpublished telephone numbers, unless you've already established a relationship. Don't use sequential dialing techniques (where the selection of prospects to be called is based on the location of their telephone number in a sequence of telephone numbers). Avoid random dialling techniques, whether automated or manual, where the identification of your prospects is left to chance. Avoid using voice-synthesized/computerized calls. Customers deserve "live" calls from reps.

Don't crowd your reps so close together that customers can hear background noise. Acoustical partitions assure privacy for your reps. Redecorate unattractive rest areas; attractive surroundings can refresh flagging spirits.

Focus on Fulfillment

Companies spend much time and money on product selection, art, copy, advertising, mailings, list rental, scripts, and telemarketing. However, if orders aren't efficiently processed, all that time and money is wasted. Jim Kobs, author of *Profitable Direct Marketing,* says firms focus on creating new products and new offers in their quest to achieve more profits. Yet, a good fulfillment process is one way to increase profitability. Kobs believes that the fulfillment department can be just as important a profit center as the marketing department. Historically, he says there has been a great deal of testing done in the planning stages, but very little testing done on fulfillment and other after-sale processes.

Fulfillment is one area you should always strive to improve. Since this is where a majority of telemarketing failures occurs, regular evaluation of the process can cut down on problems. Use the following tips to improve the fulfillment process.

- Call your center and place an order. Did you receive a letter acknowledging your order? How long did it take to receive the merchandise? Did you receive the bill before the order arrived? Was the merchandise received in good condition? If you returned the item, was the return acknowledged? Did this entire process alert you to things you never thought of before?
- Review your form letters. Do they set the right tone? Are they too wordy?
- How long does it take to resolve typical customer complaints? 24 hours? 48 hours?
- Make sure you have complete, well-defined policies and procedures for fulfillment, as well as for complaints.
- Emphasize quick fulfillment of all orders.
- Develop a good customer-service program.
- Regularly review all your forms related to fulfillment. Are any of them obsolete? Can you simplify any of them? Are they well designed?

- Tell customers if the merchandise is in stock when the order is placed. Tell them when they can expect to receive delivery.
- Never assume fulfillment orders are processed smoothly, especially if an outside vendor does your fulfillment.
- Ask yourself regularly how you can make the fulfillment process more convenient for your customers.

Designing (Almost) Failure-Proof Data Bases

Make sure your *data fields* (segments of computer memory/display used for specific purposes) are large enough to accommodate full information, especially names and addresses. Since you'll probably be "sharing" your data base, speak with your marketing and technical departments, so you'll be able to accommodate their needs. Build in a few extra data fields to allow for change and growth in your business. Your reps will be responsible for much data-entry, so use real words, not obscure computer codes, to increase their proficiency.

Put procedures in place so that the data base won't be changed for one person's or one group's sole benefit, possibly making the data base unusable for others. Once changes are agreed upon by all the key players, notify all the departments in your center of these changes.

Manual to Automated

Automation offers the advantages of increasing your overall telemarketing productivity and managing your marketing data better. The best way to deal with systems and technology is to ignore them, at least in the idea stage. Focus first on what information you need, what form it must be in, where it has to go, and how fast.

The decision to automate shouldn't arise until you've smoothed out all of the kinks in your manual system. Work on your manual setup, revising and testing the different components. Build upon the strengths of your current manual system, and eliminate its weaknesses as you get ready to automate. In the beginning, decide what best meet your needs, and determine the various reports required. During this process, form a task force, with representatives from each department. Define your requirements, and agree upon your objectives. Select your vendors. After a few team discussions, draw up a rough draft to reflect the members' needs. Ask the members to circulate the draft in their own departments to stimulate potentially valuable feedback. Team members should then approve the draft. Plan a test, correcting any problem areas, and then implement the process in phases. The work doesn't stop there. Plan for regular team reviews of the automated process. Have problems appeared that you can correct? What improvements can the team make?

Reps on Your Team

Build a strong center by including reps on your team. If reps are to do their jobs well, they must be given the power to make their own decisions.

Reps should be asked which "tools" they need to do their jobs well. If you can't use a rep's suggestion, tell the rep why. Don't alienate your reps by ignoring their ideas.

When you establish policies, develop training programs, and write training manuals, include your reps in the process. Ongoing training tells your reps that you value them as employees. Invite a rep to your management meetings or planning sessions. Rotate attendance so that each rep gets a chance to participate.

Product Fact Sheets

Product fact sheets are handy and quick guides for your reps' reference. The fact sheets eliminate the need to rummage through a reference binder or flip through computer-terminal display screens. Reps can use fact sheets, or cards, as memory joggers, or as a basis of comparison, offering customers what best serves their needs. However, the fact sheets shouldn't replace scripts. You might use a large sturdy index card to briefly list types of services, including the type of service, its benefits, features, and cost. Hang the cards on the walls, next to each rep's terminal. If you offer many products or services, print a booklet, listing only the most important facts and benefits about each service. Your scriptwriters and trainers may also find the cards helpful.

Campaign Questionnaire

After a campaign ends, distribute a questionnaire to your reps, and follow up with a group meeting to discuss their answers. This exercise will help you improve future campaigns. Ask the following questions:

Did you understand the strategy of the promotion? What other information would you have liked to receive? What were the campaign's strong points? The weak points? Did the promotion's special discount help you sell? Did the mail piece make it easier to sell the product, or more difficult? Did customers comment on the mail piece? TV commercial? Special offer? What did you like about the script? How would you have changed the script?

What would you like to see changed in future promotions? What product benefits helped you close the sale? Which objection was the most difficult one to overcome? What advice would you give to a new rep who hasn't sold this product before? Did the customers make any comments about the company that were unrelated to the products? What were the customers' main reason for buying or not buying?

What Complaints Can Tell You

Don't look at customer complaints as if they were your company's failures. View them as opportunities to establish relationships with customers, once you've resolved the complaints. A study showed that when minor complaints were resolved to the customers' satisfaction, 70% of the complainants reported that they would maintain brand loyalty. When major complaints (more than $100 loss) were satisfactorily resolved, 54% said they would maintain brand loyalty.

Complaints can alert you to rapidly changing market preferences. Complaints also provide an early warning for possible product defects, or for distribution problems. They can offer quick firsthand market intelligence. Validate the information from complaints, using a survey. Keeping track of complaints helps to determine customer satisfaction or dissatisfaction with a product. Resolving complaints can stimulate sales now and in the future. In addition, you may hear of consumers' needs for new products.

Look for Trouble

A good telemarketing manager should always be troubleshooting. Compare this year's sales figures to past years. Compare individual campaigns over the years. Take actions to improve poor performance. Monitor any newly implemented methods and practices, and be ready to adjust them again to create even more improvements. Look outside your own industry for innovative ideas to enhance your company's future. If you hear that your customers are having problems, know that their problems are your problems. Help solve your customers' problems, and you'll increase their loyalty.

Emergencies

Will you be ready when problems arise? The computers are down! Are paper order forms ready? Are printed scripts ready? Have your reps been trained to give new information about product and price changes? There's an unexpected surge in inbound calls. Do you have an "Automated Voice Response System" (AVRS) to record customer names and phone numbers, so you can call prospects back during a lull? The AVRS equipment prompts the caller to leave his name and phone number for recording, and subsequent callback. There's a sudden change in company policy that negatively affects your customers. Are your reps prepared with scripted rebuttals?

Avoid Failure in Your Customer's Eyes

Watch out for small oversights that look like failures. Don't try to sell a product to a customer who has already purchased it. Don't send direct mail with the customer's name misspelled. Don't call customers twice in one week.

If you don't promptly and correctly update a customer's address changes, he'll continue to receive billings or packages at an old address.

Be sensitive to privacy issues. Prospects with whom you have no prior relationship may resent that you've collected information about them. But, an established customer may *appreciate* that you've gathered data about his previous transactions. Don't abuse any customer information you may have.

Don't call customers who don't fit your market profile. Aim to call the best possible list, not the broadest possible list. Quality is better than quantity.

Don't put customers on hold for long periods. To customers, a few seconds on hold seems like many minutes, partly because they have nothing to do during that time.

Don't call too late at night, too early in the morning, or on holidays. Don't allow unqualified reps who are abrupt, unsure, or who don't know your products and services to call. Avoid losing incoming calls when lines are constantly busy (because you don't have a sufficient number of telephone lines). Lost calls mean lost business.

Don't transfer your customer from one department or extension to another. Cross-train your reps so that they can answer all questions. Inform your reps about new products and services. You don't want your customers to find out about them before your reps do. Coordinate field-sales and telephone-sales responsibilities so that customers aren't called by both in one day.

Speak the Customer's Language

Don't use company jargon. This is especially true of your company's acronyms. If you must use these words, explain their meaning, as a courtesy. Many customers are intimidated when they hear unfamiliar words. Eliminate these words from your form letters, and from your literature.

Weekly Trouble Report

Draw up a weekly "trouble" report to identify problems, as pointed out by your reps. Distribute these reports to the departments responsible for solving the problems. This document may prevent complaints, and it encourages communication with other departments.

Easy to Do Business With

At one company it's each employee's responsibility to make the company "easy to do business with." Whoever gets the call is responsible for the problem. The aim is to answer customer questions fully, and to resolve problems quickly. This company accomplishes this task by providing employees with several basic tools. First, a comprehensive resource book helps employees transfer customers to the proper department. A wallet-size card, distributed to employees, lists the toll-free numbers of the most frequently contacted departments, and a step-by-step process for resolving customer problems. A pocket guide expands on the information listed on the wallet-size card. Many employees willingly help customers by using these resources, or by calling an in-house number for more help.

Managers can establish similar programs at their telemarketing centers. Start simple. Gather a team of subject-matter experts and identify typical customer-contact telephone numbers or extensions. Establish procedures for customer referrals. Depending upon the number of telephone numbers, print up a simple sheet of paper, a wallet-size card, a sticker for the phone, or a booklet. Train everyone in your company about the referral process.

How to Handle Heavy Call Volume

- Have reps who handle outbound calls switch to inbound positions.
- Compile a list of reps "on call" for those heavy days.
- Use an "Automated Voice Response System" (AVRS) to record prospects' names and telephone numbers. Reps can call the respondents back during slow times.
- Cross-train reps to handle more than one campaign or product.
- If you have several centers, direct overflow to the other units. This works best with simple order-taking.
- Use past reports to analyze your center's call-volume history.
- Look for trends to better anticipate staffing needs.

Where to Find Solutions

Finding solutions to your company's problems can be as easy as listening to your reps and customers, and by keeping up with your competition.

Your frontline reps have information about what customers believe is important. Studies by Technical Assistance Research Programs (TARP) show that "frontline workers can predict 90% of problems customers will encounter, if managers would only ask in time."

During calls, encourage reps to (informally) ask customers what they expect. Instruct reps to record unsolicited responses from customers, too. Gather all this data, and rank your customers' expectations. Start to offer what your customers want. Find solutions in your customers' complaint letters, too.

Closely watch your competitors, as well. Which new products are they promoting? What do their direct-mail pieces look like? Are they targeting your top customers? What can you learn from them?

Components of an Ergonomically Pleasing Center

What do your reps see when they enter their work area? Find out for yourself by coming into your center and looking at it through a visitor's eyes.

Look at the checklist below, and add some of the "silent motivators" you may be missing. You'll increase job satisfaction, and perhaps you'll decrease turnover.

Noise control
- Acoustic panels on ceilings and wall surfaces
- Sound-absorbing wall coverings or wall hangings
- Sound-absorbing carpets
- Attractive window treatments
- Headsets for the reps

Work station
- A three-sided 5' x 7' cubicle, with 5' high panels
- Ergonomically designed chairs
- Work surface 27" to 31" from the floor
- Color-coordinated furniture in a pleasing design

Other ergonomic factors
- Nonglare lighting
- Proper air flow and temperature control
- Neutral-color walls
- Clean, attractive rest areas, cafeterias, and bathrooms
- Attractive paintings or prints on the walls
- Plants and foliage
- Adequate parking facilities

6
MOTIVATION

Have you motivated your employees today? Only if you're motivated yourself can you motivate others. It's up to you to keep your attitude in top shape. You need to face each morning determined to be a "motivation mover." Remember, your behavior is contagious. You have the power to make it a great day for all of your reps. Opportunities are everywhere to help you create a high-energy environment. Smile and greet each rep, or award a certificate of achievement. *You're* the motivator!

Motivation shouldn't be hauled out and dusted off for the monthly sales-recognition meeting. It shouldn't be something you think of only when sales are good. Motivation is the very life force of a successful telemarketing center. It is ongoing, one-on-one, and should be carefully integrated into the operating philosophy of your company. Each time your reps answer a call, your company's reputation is tested. Keep your reps "primed" for success by *motivating* them!

After you've read this chapter, write down a new motivational idea you can immediately implement.

Three Basic Principles

What exactly *is* motivation? Robert W. Pike, in his *Creative Training Techniques Handbook*, defines it as "what incites a person to action. Motive/action: Motivation is a motive for acting, a reason for doing what we do." Pike suggests three basic principles.

- You can't motivate other people. However, you can create a climate or environment in which a person is self-motivated. Answer this question for your people: "What's in it for me?" What benefit will I gain if I behave this way? If I learn this information?
- All people are motivated. They may not be motivated for the same reasons we want them to be, but they're motivated. The key is to find out what turns them on.
- People do things for their own reasons, not for your reasons. Their reasons fulfill their own self-interest.

Keep these three principles in mind as you develop your motivation programs, campaign kickoffs, contests, and training classes.

Questions

As you plan or revise your motivation program, ask yourself the following questions: How's my own attitude lately? Do I have a "can-do" attitude? If I don't, how can I develop it in my people? What is my enthusiasm level? Do my center's activities turn me on? Am I solution-oriented?

Begin motivating your reps by taking the following actions:

Create a need in your reps. Your reps are always asking, "What's in it for me?" Fill their need for a benefit by telling them *why* they need this (or that) information—how they'll benefit from it, and how they'll use it in a practical way.

Develop and maintain the interest of your reps. Create variety and add surprises in their daily work life.

Encourage healthy competition that focuses on self-improvement. Become excited yourself. Your excitement will generate group excitement.

Regularly give encouragement, recognition, and approval. Give reps a choice. Employees like to feel that they have control of their lives. When you allow them to make choices, they feel that they have that control. In the end, you'll gain their cooperation.

Motivational Program

An ongoing motivational program is a necessity in your telemarketing center. This includes motivating sales reps as well as customer-service reps. Ideally, at least one person (depending upon your center's size) should be dedicated solely to the program. If you try to add the responsibility of motivation to the manager's or the supervisor's other duties, your program may bump along unevenly. Encourage your reps to constantly build good attitudes and motivation, and this requires a full-time (and special) person. Choose your motivational manager carefully. Look for a self-motivated, high-energy person who's creative and always on the lookout for new ideas.

Jump-Start Your Motivational Program

Appoint a committee to work on motivation. Include a good representation of employees, from top to bottom, especially reps—they usually have the best ideas. Your motivational manager can head the committee. Rotate committee members to keep the ideas fresh and ever-flowing. Give the committee a catchy name. Set realistic goals for your program. Don't demotivate the committee, nor the employees they represent. Make sure the program's objectives are clear to everyone.

Discover what motivates your people by sending out a short survey, by holding meetings with small groups, or through casual conversations with your reps.

Create a theme for your program, including a logo, banners, literature, posters, and buttons. Remember, this is all about excitement. Review and revise your motivational program regularly.

Your motivational program should include a variety of specific incentive campaigns, such as daily incentives, contests, individual incentives, as well as challenging and fun incentives. Never run a yearlong campaign. People are usually only motivated for a few months, so keep those contests and specific campaigns short. When you begin a very successful incentive campaign, run it until it reaches its peak, and then let it lapse. Don't let an idea die through overuse. Bring back the incentive campaign later, so it will appear fresh.

Creating a Motivational Environment

Managers must create and nurture a motivational environment in their centers. Make your supervisors cheerleaders and coaches; treat the reps like your star players. Encourage a flexible but controlled environment. Nurture ideas; they bring excitement. Telemarketing isn't a typical business. Don't run it like an insurance office, for example. Make the physical environment all color, light, and airiness. Get the most from your surroundings and your people, but give back, too. Make the center both rep-friendly and customer-friendly.

Focus on Your Reps

Steve Riddell, sales manager for Blue Cross/Blue Shield of Virginia's Government and Individual Business Center, believes that having the right hardware and software in place is about 25% of the formula for a well-run center. The other 75% is the human element. The key is motivating, training, and treating your reps well. Riddell offers his employees opportunity and responsibility. He maintains,

> I have low regard for those companies that run their centers like factories and treat their reps like commodities. Telemarketing centers have an obligation to their employees to take care of them and to develop them.
> During interviews, I tell my reps they are in business for themselves. They can make as little or as much as they want to.

The main trait that Riddell looks for when hiring is high motivation. In return, Riddell believes he offers his reps transferrable skills that exceed what's required for the move to the next step in his company. Why does he do this? Riddell believes that, "If you open up a vision for your employees, they will want to stay longer." His theory works. He currently gets twenty applications from employees in his own company for every vacant rep position in his center.

He receives so many applications because the job pays well, and because of the environment he regularly cultivates in the center.

> I like the atmosphere to be light, exciting, with a buzz of activity in the air, so that reps will never know what will happen next. I want my reps to work in a place that is fun. You can't beat people into doing a good job. They will get even.

To keep the excitement going, Riddell walks through the center three or four times a day, sometimes to pat someone on the back, or just to sweep out the boredom.

How's Your Motivation?

Is your attitude worth catching, or has your motivation been flagging lately? Maybe you need to try something different on the job. A telemarketing manager has to create excitement for himself with new plans, innovative ideas, and a different way of doing things. However, you aren't alone in this endeavor. Share ideas with other managers through telemarketing conferences and association meetings. Read telemarketing trade magazines and books.

A Suggestion from Tom Peters

In his book *Thriving on Chaos*, Tom Peters states,

> Well-constructed recognition settings provide the single most important opportunity to parade and reinforce the specific kinds of new behavior one hopes others will emulate.

Peters suggests offering "a menu of recognition devices." Begin with informal recognition by throwing casual parties. These events needn't take much effort, nor do they have to be time-consuming. Peters gives an example of purchasing two dozen doughnuts as an "award" to a team for successfully completing a crucial part of a project on schedule. Hand out small gifts, or set up a special buffet in the lunchroom. From small recognitions, advance to recognition on a grand scale—an annual sales meeting at an elegant hotel.

What Demotivates

Poor working conditions Too much noise or crowding can wear your employees down.

No compensation program

Lack of career opportunities Whether they have supervisory aspirations, or they're interested in career advancement to other departments in your company, encourage your employees.

Poor management attitude Does upper management view the reps as important parts of the organization?

Boredom

Customer complaints or rejection As a manager you can't control this, but you can teach your reps to get back on the phones and to focus on the next call and future sales. Teach reps not to take things personally.

Idea-Killers

Idea-killers are everywhere: top and middle managers, supervisors, trainers, reps, scriptwriters, and programmers. Ditkoff and McHugh, in *The Idea*

Development Book, wrote, "It's always so much easier to say 'no' to a new idea than to consider the unexplored possibilities." Ideas are innocent until proven guilty. Be wary when you hear the following idea-killers.

- It won't work.
- We've tried that before.
- It's not practical.
- We've never done that before.
- It's not company policy.
- Why don't you form a committee?
- Maybe next year.
- We're not quite ready for that.
- We've already got enough problems here.
- When will you find the time to do it?
- Let's think about it some more.
- We've done all right without it.
- Who else has tried it?
- Why bother?
- It's already been done.
- The boss wouldn't go for it.

Supervisor's Motivational Toolbox

Goals Goals for reps should be in writing, very specific, measurable, contain deadlines, and include action plans. As a manager, you should have your own goals in writing—goals that you'll share with the reps. Many experts suggest carrying your goals with you, printed on small cards.

Training Have you ever heard of an overtrained rep? Training should be happening all the time, and not just in the classroom.

Feedback Feedback shows that you have an interest in your reps. This interest will encourage them.

Recognition A simple greeting, using the rep's name, or even a compliment are good motivators.

Meetings Quick ten-minute meetings build bonds in your group, and energize the center.

Provide benefits, both big and small, to your reps. When you provide employees with good working conditions, good pay, and top-notch training, you'll broadcast a positive message about your business, and about the telemarketing industry as a whole. Employees also care about their jobs when they know that their managers consider these jobs to be important. Adding paintings and eye-catching graphics to the walls can give reps the feeling of working in a high-quality environment. Add a competitive salary, ample parking, variety of career options, a comfortable lounge, opportunities to be part of a team, and monotony breakers, and you'll soon decrease employee turnover.

Banish Burnout

Combat employee burnout by making the job interesting and exciting, with challenges, rewards, and reachable goals. Rid your center of these causes of burnout:

- Low pay
- Lack of training
- Rejection by customers
- Lack of product knowledge
- Lack of career options
- Lack of challenges
- Poor working conditions
- Lack of recognition
- Monotony and boredom
- Lack of supervision

Replace these causes of burnout with the following activities and practices: Hire the right employees by spending time on the hiring process. Practise job rotation, so that employees learn new skills. Offer job-enrichment activities. Have reps give presentations to upper management, take visitors on tours, attend seminars, or train new reps. Encourage ongoing and advanced training. Provide handy, updated information when products and prices change. Encourage two-way communication. Let reps tell you what they need to do their job better, how they handled specific calls, and what they want their next job to be.

Take responsibility for good campaign planning to avoid those long hours spent trying to fix short-sighted plans. Set realistic schedules for everyone. Regularly show your reps that you appreciate them. Learn from your reps and implement their ideas. Award prizes for the best suggestions. No matter what the task, try doing it differently. Create career paths. Let the reps know that they constitute an important resource pool from which your company will draw. Use every opportunity to spotlight your reps. Put employees' photos in your internal newsletter. For their outstanding work, award a small group with lunch with the company president, or with a special field trip. Give employees the opportunity to influence decisions that affect them.

Be a facilitator, challenger, communicator, delegator. Don't be afraid to give up some authority; in the end, you'll get even more back from your reps.

Compensation and Contests

Compensation is your long-term motivator, and contests are short-term motivators. Design a risk/reward compensation program which combines salary (the reward) with a commission on each sale for every dollar sold (the risk). Or, you could develop a multi-tier pay structure, where each level demands a different production quota. Allow reps to pick the level they're comfortable with. Give them the option to change their choice once a month.

Contests motivate for two reasons. They change the daily routine and they help eliminate boredom, pressure, and tension. Contests imply competition, and ultimately recognition.

Plot out a weekly or monthly plan for changing the pace at your center and for recognizing and publicizing your reps' special efforts.

Two Motivational Techniques

At one company's computer-systems technical-services center, employees support large national companies who have purchased the company's computer equipment. The center receives about 1.1 million trouble reports a year. Incoming calls are first received by call-receipt agents, who then transfer the problems on for engineers to resolve. Several techniques are used to motivate employees. Two are described below.

Agent empowerment

When agents receive a call, they can attempt to solve the customer's problem immediately instead of referring the call to a subject-matter expert.

There are two benefits to this empowerment. It encourages the agent to learn more about the products, and the contact is less expensive because it doesn't tie up an expert's time. Because of their expertise, some call-receipt agents are promoted.

"Wall of Fame"

One entire wall of the center is a "Wall of Fame," where employees are recognized for customer service, revenue generation, outstanding attendance, customer agent of the month, and the top call-receipt team.

Coaching

Don't teach, don't admonish, don't scold. Coach your team to success by treating them with respect.

Help your reps sell by providing easy-to-use reference materials. Hold training update sessions. Keep your reps informed of any changes in products or prices. Create a helpful atmosphere for coaching. Provide high-quality tools and materials.

Put the Rep on Your Team

Reps' input and participation are both vital, and should be encouraged. As manager, support openness and risk-taking by creating the proper environment. Play the role of the facilitator, not the authoritarian. Allow reps to suggest new ideas and to offer solutions for problem areas. Involve reps in the decision-making process. This reinforces their importance to the organization, and enables you to rely on your employees' expertise. Try the following activities:

You'll boost morale when you, or trainees, say to senior reps, "Teach me how to do it." Make a positive impact on productivity by asking the reps what they enjoy doing, and what their personal goals are. Help reps act on their interests and goals. Have reps help design monitoring forms.

Share company goals, department goals, and specific campaign goals with your reps. Give them clear job descriptions. Give them the power to make those small decisions that build self-esteem. For example, they can solve a customer's complaint while still on the line. Give good feedback, by first telling your employees what their top skills are, and then by telling them the areas that need work. Let reps help set policies.

Get your reps involved when you develop new training programs, or ask for their input on the rough drafts of revised training manuals.

When your company exhibits at a trade show, let reps participate. Not only is this a motivator, it also gives your reps confidence. Suggest that the reps invite their customers to stop at the exhibit booth to get better acquainted. This strengthens the customer/rep relationship; you'll also increase the customer's confidence and trust in your people and products.

When quarterly sales results come out, give a presentation to your reps. Try a different approach to a persistent problem. At one center, many employees reported to work late. After a little probing, the manager learned that the reps found it difficult adhering to the rigid schedule of the center. Some wanted early hours, others wanted late hours, or a multitude of in-between hours. One rep volunteered to establish a flextime schedule for the center, and the situation was solved.

When your motivation plan doesn't seem to be working, bring the problem to your reps and put them in charge of motivation for a specific time period. The results may lead you to appoint a permanent rep-motivation committee.

If your turnover rate is high, carefully reevaluate your training programs. Are you spending enough time and care on training? Poorly trained reps tend to drop out quickly.

Focus Groups

Can you get any good ideas from focus groups? Simply organized, a focus group consists of a facilitator who guides the group discussion while adhering to a written outline. The group is small, usually consisting of eight to ten people. Experiment with different group sizes to determine the size that best meets your needs.

Draw up an outline to use as a tool for gathering the reps' insights, but be flexible. Controlling a focus group defeats its purpose. You'll find that ideas and groups don't always work out the way you expect. Be prepared to discard the notions you brought in with you.

The sessions should be short—forty-five to ninety minutes. If your meeting runs too long (more than two hours), people in the group will start to reinforce each other, thinking and reacting as a group, rather than as individuals.

Don't let one or two people dominate the conversation and bully the other participants into accepting their ideas. A good moderator should elicit responses and activity from all of the members.

Key people (managers or trainers) should observe the sessions, depending upon the subjects discussed. The best response you get from these sessions is often nonverbal. Body language can show real enthusiasm, apathy, or strong opposition. It's difficult to portray subtle responses in a written report. When you aren't in the focus group, you don't really know what happened.

Use pictures, actual products, premiums, or a prototype of the object you're discussing. Negative feedback is as important as positive feedback, especially to identify potential problems. Focus groups are designed specifically to stimulate ideas and to give your program direction. They can also initiate needed research. These sessions help reduce, not eliminate, risks in decision-making. Focus groups are limited in scope; they're not conclusive, since the size of your sample is usually small.

A written report should be compiled after the focus session ends. You may also want to videotape or audiotape the sessions.

You can gain much from holding focus groups with reps. From speaking with them, you may learn that one of your scripts is too long, or that another script is confusing. Reps can help identify faulty logic flows in sales presentations.

Campaign Kickoffs

A kickoff before a new campaign is a must. The event energizes the center. Decorate the work area to provide a festive atmosphere.

Perhaps you could create a theme: a fifties party, or even a beach party. Serve refreshments and give small gifts to the reps. A drawing for a door prize might also be tried. The kickoff is an opportune time to present your campaign strategy to the group, show the new TV commercial, and pass out sales kits. The kits should contain samples of direct-mail pieces, print ads, and the brochures you're offering to your customers. The kit can be used as a reference source during the campaign to refresh the reps' memory of the product and to answer customers' specific questions.

Telesales Contest

The manager of one large telemarketing center keep his reps motivated by using "telesales contests." A committee of volunteer reps is granted total responsibility for running these contests. Their tasks include developing a contest theme, finding a way to track sales, picking the actual products to promote, and posting daily results. They even promote the event using posters and flyers. The company's marketing staff offers advice about which products to sell, script suggestions, probing questions, and responses to objections.

Quiet Room

In the frenetic environment of a telemarketing center, who can resist a "quiet room"? One large company has a "quiet room," totally set apart from the lounge. Instead of overhead lighting, there are homey lamps. The room is dim and comfortable. No eating, drinking, smoking, or talking is allowed. The room is a haven where reps can enjoy a break in peace and quiet.

Motivate by Walking Around

Check the mood in your center by routinely walking through the work areas. This old tactic works. Here is where you'll find potential mood-spoilers. One negative or cynical rep can upset the people around him. Walk around and you'll be able to hear reps who are impolite or abrasive to customers. You want to stop these behaviors immediately. Walk through your center often, smiling, giving tips, and motivating your reps.

Have You Manned the Phones Lately?

A manager will have an entirely different perspective if he's manned the phones—personally experiencing rejection, boredom, burnout, and low sales. If you've never manned the phones, or if you haven't lately, do it now to give you insight into your reps' concerns, and you'll earn the respect of your employees, too. Your example will also motivate them.

Igniter Phrases

Lou Tice, cofounder of The Pacific Institute, a private educational corporation, believes that people have an unlimited potential for growth. His video programs are based on enhancing those excellent qualities that people already have. The programs offer techniques based on concepts of self-image psychology. In his programs, he offers "igniter" phrases that you may want to use.

I agree.
I looked at this last night and
  I really like it!
That's good!
Good job!
I made a mistake, I'm sorry.
Let's go!
I have faith in you.
That's the first time I've had
  anyone think of that.
That's interesting.
Things are beginning to pop!

You're on the right track.
That's a winner!
I'm glad you brought that up.
I appreciate what you've done.
See, you can do it!
Let's get right on it.
Let's start a new trend.
Great!
I know it will work.
Go ahead, try it.
We're going to do something
  different today.

I like that!
Good for you!
Congratulations!
Keep going!
Very good!
You're beautiful!
Do that again!
What good workers we are!

I'm very pleased with what you've done.
You can do it
You're in high gear!
We can always depend on you.
We can do a lot with that idea.
Keep up the good work.
Fantastic!

Add your own "igniter" phrases to this list.

Motivate Through Teaching

Offer your reps an innovative learning experience, and they won't even realize you're teaching and motivating them at the same time. Here are a few starters.

Product managers

At one telemarketing center, representatives from the various manufacturing divisions come to the center to seek input from the reps. They see the reps as excellent sources of marketing data. Telemarketing-center managers consider these visits an important part of their motivation program, because the reps recognize the role that they can play in the product-development process. At the same time, the reps learn more about the products.

Job-sharing

Give your reps the opportunity to voluntarily enroll in a job-sharing rotation program. When there are special tasks to do, the reps in the program get a chance to accept or decline a job offered. One benefit is job variety, and reps are able to develop new skills.

Product and service fairs

Training doesn't always take place in a classroom or through the printed word. At one car-rental center, management holds an outdoor car fair and picnic for the reps. The picnic lends a bit of festivity to the event.

Best Call

Tape your reps' best calls. Encourage them to listen to these calls when they need a little motivation.

Group Motivators

Individual incentives are not enough. To encourage a strong group identity, you need team activities such as parties, events, and outings. Team T-shirts, group goals, team-building exercises, team awards, and team contests all become strong motivators for cooperation and mutual support.

Meetings

At the end of a meeting, distribute evaluation forms to your reps for them to fill out. What did they like about the meeting? What improvements can be made?

Have reps take turns running meetings. Have them set the meeting date, the location, and have them draw up the agenda.

Contests

Don't set the requirements for winning so high that no one wins. The wider the appeal of a contest, the more successful it will be. After a good contest, the sales reps should be better off, and so should the company. Have a few reps help plan the contest.

Always Motivating

The responsibility for motivating your reps can be overwhelming. The challenge can also be daunting, because if you don't motivate, you lose. You have quite a job to do, and if you don't have a department or manager in your center dedicated to motivation, it's all up to you. As with any other large undertaking, breaking the project up into small tasks makes it easier. Divide your motivation program up into categories, to make it simpler to manage, and to avoid overlooking any potential areas for motivation. To develop your own program, add more ideas to those listed below.

- Create a daily atmosphere of energy and excitement by pretending it's opening day at your center.
- Treat your employees as your customers.
- Distribute a daily "news sheet" focusing on any changes affecting the campaign. During calls, a rep wants to inform the customer before the customer informs him.
- Keep "update training" modules on hand for that slow day.
- Motivate simply. A genuine smile, "Hello," and "How are you today?" are all great motivators.
- Have a weekly "dress-down" day.
- Offer free doughnuts in the morning, or free dessert at lunchtime.
- Award a free lunch to the rep (or group) with the most sales.
- Award a prize to the rep who receives the most customer compliments in a month.

- Promote quality control. If a rep has an error-free month, give him a monetary award.
- Offer a group incentive when service levels are achieved for the month.
- Hold a food party once a month.
- Catch employees doing something right. Later, write a congratulatory message and post it on their terminals or in their work area.
- When a rep receives a compliment from a customer, give the rep two tickets to the movies, or a free lunch.
- As contest prizes, award gift certificates to inexpensive local restaurants, or to local stores.
- Print elegant-looking "outstanding service" certificates, with blank lines for the dates and the rep's name.

When giving out sales awards, give out goofy gifts, too. This tactic lightens up the atmosphere, adds suspense during the ceremony, and recognizes those reps who didn't win an award. Gifts could include things like a bag of coffee beans for the person who can't function before his morning coffee.

Tom Peters, in his book *Thriving on Chaos*, described one company which holds a "zero-defect" celebration. Plan a similar program in your company by setting goals for decreasing the error rate in any of the following areas: fulfillment, billing, or the reps' input of customer data. Determine the duration of the program, such as one month. An employee committee should be able to define and handle any of the details. The committee could also identify opportunities for improvement, and suggest new procedures for streamlining processes.

Are "second attempts" in your script not working? Hold a contest and give a prize to the rep who comes up with the best "second attempt" script. Use the winning entry in your script.

Whenever a manager sees reps doing something right, or showing improvement, he can give the reps a "thumbs-up" card. The card could give the rep an extra fifteen minutes of break time, or the rep could leave work fifteen minutes early. The rep can decide when the card will be used.

If you're renovating your center, or building a new one, request the reps' input on design and color.

Stew Leonard, Sr., owner of the world's largest dairy store, doesn't use the word "employee." He prefers to say "team member." He likes to give his team members dignified titles for their jobs that make them proud to tell others what they do and where they work. Leonard even gives everyone (from assistant manager on up) personalized calling cards. They can hand out these cards when they boast about their jobs.

Recognition

Teach reps to believe in offering value-added service to their customers. Reward them for doing so with cash awards, recognition in company newsletters, an inexpensive trip, or an annual bonus. For perfect attendance, treat reps to lunch in a restaurant.

Spotlight your recently promoted reps on an "Up the Ladder" bulletin board. The company newsletter offers recognition, participation, cooperation, and feedback, and it's also an indirect educational tool.

Give a rep an actual token for an exceptional sale. A fixed number of tokens equals a prize.

Never underestimate the power of recognition for motivating employees. Recognize reps with what they want: money, a promotion, time off, a plaque. You don't know what they want? Ask them!

Take photos of events at your center and post them on a bulletin board for all to see. Halfway through a tough campaign, hold a "rep appreciation" day. Provide refreshments and small gifts.

If your center is open on holidays, or the day before a holiday, bring in a holiday meal. Recognize employees' birthdays and service anniversaries.

Hang a twenty-dollar bill on the bulletin board. The rep with the most sales that day wins the money. Play "pass the gift." Hand a gift to a rep to hold for the moment. Periodically, announce that it's time to pass the gift to the next rep. Do this a few times until the gift is passed around. Finally, announce that whoever has the gift at that moment keeps it. Don't play favorites.

Campaign Countdown

To keep a high energy level during the last two weeks of a sales campaign, have a printer make up a few large calendars listing the calling days remaining in the campaign in descending order. The dates should be printed in large black bold letters and numbers, with a tear-off sheet for each day. Start with day fourteen. Hang the calendars throughout the center. Every day, have a dramatic ceremony, tearing off the previous day's sheet. Have a celebration at the end of the campaign.

Point of No Return

If you try to cut call length too drastically, you'll rob reps of their time and creativity, and they may become apathetic. Yet, lengthy calls are expensive. Careful balance is the key to success.

Toughest Call of the Day

For reps, the toughest call to make can be the first call in the morning. Encourage your outbound reps to begin the day successfully by calling the customer most likely to place an order.

Keep the Motivation Moving

Keep reps excited and guessing about what your next motivational program will be. Be receptive to the many ideas around you.

Sustain Your Stars' Interest

What do you do with your star reps to keep them motivated? Let them devote 10–15% of their work time to "outside" projects, including script-writing or auditing records.

One-Idea Club

Stew Leonard realized that the best way to compete with other grocery stores was to relentlessly implement new ideas. He developed the "One-Idea" club, made up of managers who travel to supermarkets throughout the country. Members must return with one idea that they champion and put into effect within forty-eight hours, and they must, in turn, leave the host company's personnel with one idea to use. Negative impressions of other businesses are never discussed.

Try a variation of the "One-Idea" club with your managers and supervisors. Talk to other telemarketing-center managers to get the idea exchange going. If visiting other centers isn't feasible, send your supervisors to one-day telemarketing seminars, conferences, and classes, and require them to come back with at least one idea they can implement within forty-eight hours. Make this a requirement for yourself, too. The one-idea theory is achievable and productive.

Motivation File

Start a motivation file. Write your ideas on file cards, and separate the cards into categories, using tab dividers. Categories might include any of the ideas mentioned in this chapter. You might put in additional categories, such as campaign-kickoff ideas, awards, top performers, low performers. The categories should be in line with the needs of your center. Carry a pocket-size notepad or tape recorder with you to capture your thoughts. Review your cards, discard the weak ideas, and add new ideas.

Fear of Calling

Fear can affect both new and seasoned reps. To overcome this, "fear of calling" should be addressed during the first days of training. Provide ongoing support to experienced reps so that they won't experience this fear. Fear of calling is a fear of being rejected.

Joel Linchitz, author of *The Complete Guide to Telemarketing Management*, lists the most typical fears in the rep's mind.

Rejection Will the person I've called say "No," or even hang up on me?

Qualification fear Am I speaking to the person who has the authority to decide?

Time fear Do I have enough time to get the important points across?

Objection fear Am I understanding this person's real objections?

Sales fear Can this sale be made? Can I make it? How much should I sell?

Closing fear Is it time to close?

Linchitz maintains that the prospect may be experiencing similar feelings, with the following questions running through his mind.

- Why is this person calling me?
- How long will it take?
- Can I trust this person?
- Do I need more information?
- Should I make this decision alone?
- How can I shortcut this process?
- Can I afford to do this?
- Can I change my decision later?

To break down some of the psychological barriers to telephone communications, Linchitz recommends the following steps. Most of these can be done before the first call is made.

- Limit carefully whom your calls must reach. Define your market.
- Decide what to expect from each market segment. Make test calls *first*.
- Find out what excites the individuals you call, and what ignites their desire to buy. Make sure these "hot buttons" are in the scripts you develop for each population segment.
- Be sure you can deal with the worst. Practise and role-play, particularly worst-case scenarios, to confront your fears.
- Make enough calls. Getting your message across enough times is what matters. Be sure you know how much is enough.

Look for symptoms of "call reluctance." Your reps may delay the first call of the day. They may not follow up on sales leads, or they may make few calls per hour. Discuss "fear of calling" during training, your refresher classes, and during team meetings. Discuss possible causes. Is it the particular campaign, or the personality types the reps are calling?

During meetings, encourage reps to share their feelings and to give examples of how they can overcome fear of calling. Provide reps with practical suggestions on how to deal with this fear.

Whatever the root cause, intensive role-play, focusing on objections, can prepare reps for live calls. The greater the range of experience you provide in training, the abler your reps will be to counter call reluctance.

Running Out of Ideas?

Hold a contest to initiate new motivation programs! Give prizes for the best incentive programs devised by your reps. By using the reps' ideas, you'll gain their acceptance. A motivation contest keeps the motivation ideas fresh. The goals and objectives of the center become real to the reps. The reps understand why incentive programs are important. The job becomes more interesting to your employees. The contest breaks the routine and adds variety. At the start of the contest, hold a short workshop on incentive programs.

Words of Motivation

Try posting some of these ideas on a bulletin board, or on the reps' computer terminals.

- Motivation = *Motiva*te for ac*tion*
- The most powerful ideas often receive the greatest resistance.
- Change is uncomfortable.
- To achieve, you must compete against yourself.

A month's worth of motivation ideas

- Once reps have produced their daily quotas, let them go to the lounge, or let them go home, with pay.
- Allow reps to choose their own part-time schedules. This keeps the reps happy and reduces absenteeism.
- If your meetings are predictable, they're boring. Use music, humor, videos, posters, interesting props, "icebreaker" exercises.
- Don't let the same people win the contests all the time; other reps might stop trying. Reward things other than sales—best customer service call, error-free order input, top number of cross-sales, most knowledgeable rep, top team player.
- Spend time giving positive feedback to reps.
- Write a personal note to one of your reps.
- Award reps for going above and beyond the call of duty.
- After a tough campaign, award reps and their significant others with a free night of dinner and dancing.
- Plaques, televisions, telephones, and answering machines are all good prizes. These awards will always remind the reps of the reward for excellence; they also reinforce positive feelings towards the company.
- Link the incentive awards to the performance you wish your reps to achieve, such as new leads or closed sales.
- Let reps earn and accumulate points to provide them with gifts from a catalog.
- Tell your vice president when a rep has had a great sales month, and have him send a note or flowers to the rep.
- Tell reps exactly what you want them to achieve.
- Give immediate awards for achievement, on the spot.
- Let reps nominate each other for awards.
- Give your best reps the work stations near the windows. Or, award the window seats as prizes.

- Remember that your younger reps may prefer awards that differ from those your older reps might like.
- Feature reps in your commercials, brochures, promotional literature, and training videos.
- Every day, and in every way, create high energy, variety, and excitement.
- Run incentive programs that allow for multiple winners. For example, a contest that awards a prize to everyone who meets a certain level of performance. This will give even your low performers a chance to win and gain recognition. This is a good motivator for new employees.
- Announce that prizes will be awarded to the three reps who make the highest number of sales within the next hour.
- Using a large electronic screen, display the total number of sales for the day, changing the numbers on the screen as the sales increase.
- If your center usually runs several campaigns at the same time, separate your reps into teams. This promotes a sense of "ownership" as the reps work towards the campaign's success. This can also instill friendly competition within and among the teams. Print team T-shirts.
- Treat your employees the way you'd like them to treat your customers.
- Choose a creative theme for your individual incentive programs.
- Ask one of your trainers to give a one-hour workshop on motivation. Topics to be covered could include self-esteem, winning skills, stress management, creativity, and success.
- Award paper tokens to reps for meeting specific goals. Tell the reps to deposit their tokens in a large box. The more goals reps have met, the more tokens they'll have in the box, and the greater their chance of winning a weekly drawing.

7
TRACKING

A telemarketing center's progress, campaigns, and results all need to be tracked, measured, and tested. Ongoing review keeps your center healthy. Not only does analysis help you effectively manage your campaigns, but it alerts you to potential problems before they escalate. To make sure that measurement is an ongoing process in your center, set up a yearly schedule. Set specific dates when center teams can conduct various kinds of reviews. A specific review schedule will ensure that reviews get done regularly during the year. When developing an annual review schedule, set a date for a complete operations review.

Scan daily reports. Intensely test pilot programs, to find out what you can learn from them. A pilot program, properly tested, can save you money, time, and mistakes. Teach *everyone* the importance of measurement. Reps can be taught to track their own performance, and to set objectives. After you've developed your annual measurement and tracking schedule, review it. Pass it around to other departments. Are there other areas that need to be tracked, but aren't reflected in your schedule? If there are, add them in. This chapter discusses specific areas that need to be tracked, and how to do it.

To be successful, a telemarketing center needs complete commitment from top management, and a good market plan that projects expenses, revenues, equipment, personnel needs, and a process for tracking results. There must also be adequate funding.

Center objectives should be realistic, achievable, and include both short- and long-term projections. Objectives must be based on the requirements of the marketplace. Review your center's progress every 90 days and fine-tune your program. Set standards for measuring the progress you make meeting objectives.

Tracking Reports

As with your scripts, all of your center's forms should be regularly reviewed and tested. It's easy to retain too much data, the wrong data, or meaningless data. Set up team reviews to edit all your center's forms and reports. These teams should consist of all the people who have anything to do with reports, including managers, programmers, and clients.

What You Measure Is What You Get

When you design your measuring system, realize that what you measure is what you'll get, and what will get done. If you don't effectively track an activity, you can't effectively manage it.

Let's say a center measures performance based on gross sales. Its reps will sell as many of the easy-sale products as possible, regardless of profit-per-sale. Similarly, if a center begins to measure contact attempts, reps will give it just that—attempts, not completion.

Set Realistic Goals

According to Richard L. Bencin,

> Once the concept has been developed and the basic planning of the procedures sketched out in some formalized way, the objectives or goals of the program have to be set. "Goals," as I'm referring to them here, mean measurable outcomes expected of the telemarketing program.
>
> The concept defines what we are going to do, the plan describes how we're going to do it, and the goals define how much of it we're going to achieve.
>
> Typical goals could include more appointments for the sales staff, more qualifications of sales leads, more prospecting for new business, more renewals of lapsed business, and so on, with specific quantifiable outcomes set for each goal. But goals aren't simply quantities, they also involve generous yet precise timetables for accomplishing the various portions of a task, a series of milestones that allow the program to be assessed at intervals, so midcourse adjustments and corrections can be made.
>
> Goals must be specific. With each goal, specific quantifiable dollar and/or unit targets must be set, along with achievable start-up dates.

Testing Campaigns

Along with forecasting calls, and tracking sales results, test customers' reactions to campaigns, specific products, selling methods, and creative approaches.

Test one revised section of a script, or a completely different script against your current script. Make sure tests are statistically valid. Your "control" script is what you test all other approaches against. Always test for yourself. Someone else's campaign results can't be applied to your own campaign. The markets change from year to year, so test results don't last forever. Keep on testing.

Tracking Campaigns

Regular, careful tracking lets you know when a campaign is beginning to slow down, and quickly tells you what needs fixing. Based upon cumulative totals of campaign results, you'll be able to decide knowledgeably whether to continue or expand your telemarketing program. Tracking your reports will show you hourly, daily, weekly, and monthly trends.

Your sales plan must include your goals and what it will cost you to achieve those goals—both minimum and maximum cost projections. Base your projections on what can realistically be accomplished. If your field-sales staff generally has a 25–30% close ratio, then your reps will probably have a 15–18% close ratio. If your reps sell an expensive product, expect them to make two to three contacts for each close. These ratios and contact rates will vary, depending upon your business.

Sales volumes can, many times, be overestimated because of a manager's incorrect assumptions. Faulty assumptions include: the contact/close ratio is underestimated, the flow of reorders is difficult to establish over the telephone, the receptivity of the market is overestimated, or the product is nearing maturity.

Monitoring Your Center's Performance

Personnel How do managers interact with reps? What is employee turnover? Absenteeism? What's the background of your management team? What are your labor policies?

Scripts Are your scripts being used? Do they need to be reviewed or rewritten?

Monitoring Is monitoring being used effectively?

Call accounting Can rep telephone-connect time be quantified per telephone hour, per day?

Productivity reports Can call attempts, sales presentations, completed calls, and sales per hour be accounted for?

Marketing–analysis reports Can your center determine the best selling sequence for the most productivity? Which list, script, mailer, or offer is the most effective? Is it more productive to use part-time or full-time reps?

Quotas Are sales quotas used? Are they reasonable? Do managers and reps understand the importance of quotas?

Business Sales Cycle

In business-to-business telemarketing, you'll usually have to make many calls before you're able to close a sale. Tracking results at the beginning of the sales cycle may give you an unrealistic view of performance to date. During the first week, your reps concentrate on their first contacts. Consequently, sales and percentage of sales to your goal will be low.

Three Essential Outbound Telemarketing Reports

- The *Program Status Report* tells you how your overall campaign is performing. This report should include work hours, on-line hours, off-line hours, dials, contacts, sales, dollar volume of sales, not available, no answers, bad numbers, not interested, send literature, and sales as a percentage of goal.

- The *Rep Report* is similar to the status report, but all numbers are tracked for each individual rep. Compare each rep's productivity to the group's.
- The *Profitability Report* matches expenses to revenue generated. Compile this report daily, weekly, and monthly.

Tracking

Track reports daily. Use these reports to set daily goals and as a means to spot potential problems. An Automatic Call Distributor (ACD) can quickly provide detailed marketing data.

Experts recommend tracking the following data, using either an automated or a manual system.

- Total call volume
- Calls handled per rep
- Calls per 800 number
- Peak calling hours and seasonality
- Number of busy signals received per caller
- Area codes from which calls originate
- Length of time callers are put on hold
- Time of day calls are received by the center
- Average overall sales
- Call abandonment rate (customers hang up before they reach a rep)
- Off-hour transactions
- Total number of transactions per rep
- Names, addresses, and phone numbers of callers
- Caller's purchasing history
- Dollar value of sales per rep
- Credit-card data
- Special promotions
- Prospect and customer profiles
- Number of rings preceding an answer

What Can Reports Do for You?

Reports can provide the number of inbound calls by half-hour segments, indicating high calling peaks in a day, or a week. Reports can track the number of inbound "abandoned" calls, pointing out the times when more reps need to be working. Reports can indicate how much work is left to do in an outbound campaign. Track the number of employees hired or terminated in a year. Tracking training hours will enable you to manage your training costs. Use reports to help you document rep performance and indicate which reps need the most help; these rep reports can be used when you evaluate your reps. Reports can record the number of sales per script, customer objectives, and they can document why customers aren't buying.

Help Reps Set Goals

Work with your reps to set goals. Encourage your reps to focus on the different parts of a call, and to set daily goals for dials, contacts, average call length, closes, and close ratio. On a monthly basis, ask reps to monitor their career, financial, and productivity goals.

Set Objectives for Your Business Calls

Set objectives for each business call in order to track rep productivity.

First contact During this call the rep introduces himself and your company, qualifies the customer, determines the company's decision maker, and sends requested information. If the opportunity arises, he closes the sale.

Second contact During this follow-up call, the rep asks for the order.

Third contact If you haven't done so yet, close the sale, or remove the customer from the list, or schedule future follow-up calls.

Four typical "peak" periods in an inbound center

Hourly peaks During certain hours of the day, there will be peak periods in your center. By careful tracking of your daily reports, you'll notice a pattern. Use these patterns to project inbound calls. Peaks also depend upon the media used (direct-response TV, direct mail), and the target audience.

Consumer telemarketing peaks are not as consistent from program to program as are business telemarketing peaks.

Business-to-business telemarketing usually generates two peaks: midmorning and midafternoon. However, if business calls are received from different time zones, the peaks even out.

In the case of mail and print, nonemployed customers (retirees, homemakers) generate peaks midmorning, midafternoon, and early evening. Employed customers cause peaks during the early evening on weekdays, and during the day on weekends.

Daily peaks In the business-to-business weekday operation, Monday will be the heaviest response day, with nearly one-quarter of the total weekly response. On Tuesday, volume will diminish. Wednesday and Thursday will be the slowest days. Volume builds up again on Friday.

In consumer programs, peak days are usually Saturdays and Sundays. However, much depends on when the promotion begins. A Sunday-newspaper insert will cause peaks on Sunday and Monday. Response will trail off on Tuesday. Managers should be aware that there are many other variables that affect inbound volume, other than the four peak periods discussed here. Rather than relying on set expectations, a manager should be constantly on the lookout for variables, and he should adjust his projections accordingly.

Seasonal peaks Every company has seasonal peaks. Determine these peaks by tracking call data for several years.

Promotion peaks Promotion peaks depend upon the medium used. If you use catalogs, the peak is three to six weeks after the catalog is mailed. With direct mail, the peak is one to three weeks after mailing. Direct-response TV is usually the most difficult medium to manage. Heavy peaks will occur up to one half-hour after the commercial's airing.

How to Better Manage Your Center's Inbound Service Level

- Have reps specialize, handling only one campaign, one geographic area, one type of customer (retail industry, computer industry, etc.). This makes for personalized service.
- Revamp and improve your training program.
- Cross-train your reps so that they can handle calls from other campaigns when the incoming call volume rises.
- Broadcast any changes in a campaign using the reps' computer terminals.
- When inbound-call volume is heavy, have a backup team ready. Cross-utilize your reps, or maintain a list of reps "on call."
- Offer a voluntary furlough option. When call volume is low, allow reps to go home, and pay them for a full day.

Measure Your Reps' Productivity

Rather than measuring the specific number of calls a rep handles, try the following techniques: Was the rep signed into the computer system for the same amount of time as was shown on his time card? Was the rep's average call length within your organization's standards? Was the sales ratio within the range of your standards? If the rep meets these requirements, he's productive.

Setting Objectives for a New Campaign

With outbound promotions, don't set objectives for a new campaign before it begins. Use the first three to seven days to closely track all results, using daily reports.

Call a combination of your best and worst prospects. Compare the results to past campaigns, taking into consideration the variables of each promotion. You should be ready to project the total number of sales, completions per hour, and conversion rate of calls to sales. Continue to compare your results with your projections.

Tracking your inbound promotions by half-hour segments, and comparing results to the previous weeks' data and past campaigns, will show that a pattern emerges. Patterns can even be found in "run-of-station" airings. (TV stations run a commercial when open time is available.)

Testing

First write down your test strategy, showing the objective of the test, and detailing how it will be carried out.

To effectively measure the progress of a campaign, set up *test cells* during the planning process. Which cells to test?

Control cells Measure a "known" response direct-mail campaign (with no telephone follow-up) against the same mailing *with* a telephone follow-up.

Mailing lists Measure the effectiveness of one mailing list against another.

Offer Measure the responses to different offers. For example, compare a service you've promoted with no enrollment fee versus a service *with* a fee.

Other variables to measure include your customers' life-styles, your customers' social and economic characteristics, and consumer sensitivity to price changes.

Carefully analyze and weigh test cell results to determine which test cell gave the best statistically valid results.

Set Campaign Standards

Setting necessary standards can give you something to measure against. For example, what's necessary to achieve profits? Four sales per hour? Or, will you measure by revenue-per-hour? Other objectives to measure include completed contacts per hour, number of prospects not reached, number of incorrect telephone numbers/names, percentage of contacts to sales, number of callbacks, and the number of printed pieces mailed.

Forecast Inbound Calls

The key to accurate forecasting is to effectively combine quantitative and judgmental factors. You'll never completely eliminate the uncertainties and inaccuracies inherent in forecasting. However, you'll be successful if you compare your forecasts to your actual results, and try to determine why there's a discrepancy. Experience and the results of past campaigns will also help you to refine your forecasting skills.

Determine the total number of calls your center will receive. Break down this number into seasonal, monthly, weekly, daily, and half-hour segments. Look for calling patterns; tracking and analyzing historical data will aid you. No matter what the campaign, calling patterns almost always exist, and this is the data you'll use to forecast.

During weeks with holiday closings, adjust your data. For example, the day that follows a three-day weekend presents a challenge to forecasting. Calling patterns can also be affected by regularly scheduled events, such as billing cycles (when your company sends out bills) or when your company mails its advertising.

To estimate the number of calls your inbound center can handle, try this:

Forecast your center's calls, estimating down to the half-hour. Estimate the average talk time per call. Add in the average after-call work time.

According to Bencin, it's usually necessary to follow the results of a program for a number of months before any real evaluation can be made. This long-term follow-up is necessary, not only to generate data to justify the particular program, but also to discover ways to increase sales and to generate ideas for improving the program.

Perhaps some customers don't pay. Others might be "multibuyers," or they reorder frequently. It may be wise to step up your sales efforts to certain customers, or to send them additional mail, catalogs, or to invite them to special meetings, demonstrations, or periodic sales.

Tracking is essential in order to maintain complete control of the telemarketing program. Properly done, tracking enables the manager to respond quickly to unexpected resistance, and to take advantage of marketing opportunities while they're still opportunities.

8

NOT WORKING

You spent the last few weeks putting in twelve-hour days; you checked and rechecked. In fact, everything looked good on the first day of the campaign, but now results are slipping. The campaign's not working. Your first reaction might be to kill the campaign immediately. Sometimes this is just what you'll have to do. Before you take that step, do some analysis, ask some questions, or initiate a contingency plan. By working through a tough campaign, you'll gain some valuable knowledge that will serve you well in the future.

When a campaign begins to flounder, take some aggressive corrective action. Throw in some new ideas. To add a fresh perspective, bring in people from other departments who are new to the campaign. Form a special "action" team to put in a few days of intensive effort to resolve the problems. Hold some focus groups with your reps.

Richard Bencin believes that anytime a program begins to falter, the lists should be carefully examined, the reps monitored, and the offer tested to determine what's going wrong. One of the advantages of telemarketing is the fact that its important elements (lists, representatives, offers, responses) can be altered very quickly.

This chapter suggests what to do when a campaign isn't working.

25 Questions

Something's wrong! Sales are below projection, or worse—nothing seems to be going right. Whatever their cause, problems mean that it's time to ask questions. The more you question, the closer you'll be to a solution. Listed below are some prompting questions.

- Was there total commitment from management?
- Who developed the campaign? Was there consensus among all the key players?
- Were the right reps selected for the job?
- Was ongoing daily management in place?
- If the campaign is business-to-business, were the right accounts selected?
- Were the environmental and informational needs of the reps properly and fully fulfilled?
- Were results measured properly?
- Did reps have the required forms?
- Were internal systems and departments supportive?
- Were the specific market strategies coordinated with telemarketing, direct mail, and sales-support materials?
- Were field-sales and rep-sales efforts coordinated?
- Were the reps well trained? What was the ratio of new to seasoned reps?

- Was an ongoing monitoring program in place?
- What kind of incentive program was there for the reps?
- If this was an outbound campaign, was there a good reason for the call?
- Was there sufficient name recognition for the product?
- Was the script too long? Confusing?
- Was the campaign carried out during the right season?
- Were people home when you called?
- Was the timing of the direct-mail drop and the subsequent outbound calls synchronized correctly?
- Was the price too high? Too low?
- Did the script convey a sense of urgency?
- How motivating was the direct-mail copy? Print ad?
- Were the reps regularly coached and motivated?
- Were customer complaints tracked, resolved, and handled in a timely manner?

Add even more questions to this list. Even if your campaign is successful, keep questioning for success.

Use Quality Service to Make It Work

When things aren't working, and the pressure is on, don't yield to the temptation to do a "quick fix." The "fix" will only work for a limited time, and then things will start to break down again. Stop, regroup, and refocus on your customers and on quality that's defined in terms of customer perception.

Many companies now implement customer-focused quality programs to make things work right the first time. This emphasis on continuous quality improvement has resulted in a wide array of theories and books about the concept. Tom Peters suggests that a company pick one system and implement it religiously. He says that it "makes little difference which system you choose . . . as long as it is thorough and followed rigorously." Peters emphasizes that "measurement is the heart of any improvement process." What gets measured, gets done.

Peters maintains that the best leaders are also the best note-takers, the best "askers," and the best learners. He encourages theft, too, trading the phrase "not invented here" for "not invented here, but swiped from the best with pride." Peters asks, "Will it work (with a twist or two) for us?" Former Citytrust President Jon Topham has a similar attitude. "Somebody, somewhere, big or small, near or far, has introduced a service we could copy with enhancements— today." However, Peters states that every idea you "steal" needs to be adapted and enhanced to fit your special circumstances. He believes that "uniqueness most often comes not from a breakthrough idea, but from the accumulation of thousands of tiny enhancements that utterly transform the product and create new markets in the process."

Look at the campaign or the function that isn't working, and apply some new ideas to the problem, or borrow another center's or another industry's tactics.

Teams and Processes

According to Glenn M. Parker, author of *Team Players and Teamwork*, teamwork is an important business strategy. Working within teams, you can reduce costs, improve quality, and increase production, all the things that help you stay competitive. Teams can focus on *listening* to customers to make sure that the products and services become more valuable and useful. If you stop listening, some other company will move in to take your place. The current obsession with quality, rather than with profits, offers opportunities for company teams. Will forming a team fix your problems? You need teams, and teams can solve problems, but as Parker wisely points out, "not every group is a team and not every team is effective."

After you form the team, then comes the hard part. Peter R. Scholtes, author of *The Team Handbook*, discusses "quality leadership," a concept that "emphasizes results by working on methods. Problems are solved, not just covered up." Look at tasks in your center in a new way—as steps in a process.

Each activity in your center is part of a process, and there are thousands upon thousands of processes in every company. Since a company works through processes, you can only improve your work by improving processes. Scholtes concludes that "better processes mean better quality, which means greater productivity."

Although processes can vary widely, a general approach can be used in almost all situations.

Plan-Do-Check-Act (PDCA)

When a campaign begins to fizzle, or you start having problems with a specific department in your center, try using the "Plan-Do-Check-Act" cycle. The cycle was developed by Japanese executives in their quest for implementing quality principles in their corporations. The cycle is based on the "Deming wheel," named for the "father" of modern quality management.

The cycle begins with an analysis of the current situation; data is gathered to be used to design a plan to improve present practices. Once the plan is finalized, it's implemented. Once implementation has been completed, a check is done to determine whether the anticipated improvement has been achieved. If the experiment is successful, a final action is taken to ensure that the new methods introduced will be regularly practised for sustained improvement.

Once an improvement is made, it then becomes the standard to be challenged with new plans for increased improvement.

Although most employees in the United States view standards as fixed goals, practitioners of PDCA in Japan look at standards as the place to start to do a better job the next time around. In its simplest form, PDCA can be broken down into the following steps.

- Plan what to do.

- Do it.
- Check what you did.
- Act on the differences from the plan to prevent errors the next time.

PDCA is an easy formula to apply to those things in your center that aren't working, or to unexpected crises. Try the formula on an easy problem first. From the success you achieve, move on to bigger problems in your center.

What Isn't Working?

When a campaign begins to lose momentum, figure out exactly what it is that isn't working. Break your campaign apart piece by piece to locate the malfunction. Is the problem an operational issue? A scripting issue? The ideas below will provide you with some starting points.

Operational issues

Fine-tune your inbound and outbound programs to increase sales results. Inbound reps can put likely prospects into a follow-up queue. Outbound reps call later to clinch the sale.

If a prospect says that he wants to be called back after he reads your literature, or after he discusses the information with another person, build good customer relations by having the same rep make the callback. Track the results of this endeavor.

If you coordinate direct-mail efforts with outbound calling, identify the customers who've already ordered either by using the 800 number, or by using the coupon in the direct-mail package. You'll avoid the risk of calling someone who's just ordered the product or service.

If you offer a new product, make sure it's available in all areas where you run the promotion. If the item is something you stock or provide in-house, be sure you're ready to send it out.

Listen to what your customers say. Did customers order something and not receive it yet? Are customers billed incorrectly? How often are you hearing these complaints?

Scripting issues

Always develop and customize your script, keeping your target audience in mind. A *"cost-saving"* message may be suitable for one market, while a *"stimulation"* message may be profitable in another.

Would more probing by your reps help you to determine your customers' particular needs, and would this result in more closings?

If you promote a family of products or services, write your script so that it's easy for the rep to sell the most expensive product first, and then to move down to the less expensive product, until the sale is clinched.

Are you promoting the same campaign start and end dates in your scripts? Television? Direct mail? Or is the end date in your direct-mail piece different from the end date in your script?

Is your sales presentation given in a logical order? Tape a typical call. Listen for a logical flow to the sales conversation. Talk to your top performers about the logic flow. Revise the script as needed.

Rebuttal issues

Prepare a set of scripted rebuttals that answer the most common, anticipated customer objections to a specific campaign. Each campaign usually demands its own customized rebuttals. General rebuttals may be easier to use, but they won't help to sell your product.

If an unanticipated objection does arise, instruct your rep to respond with an answer that's related to the customer's objection. Give reps the flexibility to use their own judgment and the selling skills you taught them. If this new objection tends to occur frequently, prepare a scripted rebuttal for the reps to use.

During monitoring, record your reps' spontaneous responses to customer objections. You may want to incorporate successful responses in your future scripts.

After the Campaign

Hold rep focus groups after a campaign ends. Rep feedback can indicate which tactics did and didn't work, and can highlight areas for improvement in future campaigns, or in your products and services.

Prepare for the focus group by compiling a list of questions to which you're seeking answers, regarding the campaign. Start the focus group by asking these questions. Soon the reps will be telling you the things that need to be fixed, what the customers are asking for, and what problems the reps are experiencing. Apply this valuable information to future efforts.

"Conversion"—Turn Calls into Sales

- Try a new introduction. Drop the aggressive sales opening. Develop an introduction that shows concern for the customer; put the customer first in your script. Then try to sell to the customer.
- Escalate one-on-one monitoring and coaching of your reps, especially your top sellers.
- Set up small coaching groups; have your top reps coach less productive reps.
- Track sales "conversion" against customer profiles. Which market segments produce the highest sales?
- Decide if it's worth the higher cost-per-sale to call the low-sale market segments.

- Write a new script with an entirely new approach. Test the script on a small group of prospects. If the script is successful, use it.
- Create a new short-term, high-intensity, and high-reward incentive program to add new spirit to the campaign.
- Focus on program adaptability instead of hours and cost.
- Closely monitor your weekly "no sale" report. Do a direct-mail/ telemarketing test, promoting to those prospects who didn't purchase at the time of the initial call. Include customers who didn't purchase because they didn't perceive any cost savings. Offer them a special discount.

Contingency Plan

Always keep in mind what steps to take if things suddenly stop working. Prepare for that possibility with a contingency plan. If your computer system suddenly breaks down, do you have updated paper scripts that your reps can use? Are your reference binders in top shape? Reps will need these tools when your computer system is unavailable. What would you do if you lost important sales and tracking data? Do you have a backup system?

If a campaign must be killed due to poor sales, do you have a strategy for making up the lost revenue? What will you do if you have surplus staff? Immediately need 20 additional reps? A heavy snowfall prevents reps from getting to work? What if you run out of inventory?

Report Analysis

Study (or regularly scan) your daily, weekly, and monthly reports. By routinely working with these reports, you'll be able to catch problems before they become crises. Daily and weekly results can also indicate when it's time to intervene to save a campaign, or when to pump up sales. Weekly results will let you know if your projections are on target. A monthly report helps you analyze a campaign.

A "no sale" report, with categories indicating the reason for no sale, can tell you why a campaign is doing poorly. Categories in such a report could include "dislikes telemarketing calls" or "already owns product." The report can suggest areas to target or avoid in your next promotion.

Develop a prospect file, and monitor customer dissatisfaction. The report may indicate that you've exhausted your customer base for a certain product. Ask yourself what the "no buys" tell you, and then take steps to reverse the situation.

Selling Complex Products

A campaign may be unsuccessful because the product or service is too complex to sell by phone. A mailing, educating the prospect about the product, should be sent before making the outbound call. Depending upon product complexity, the rep can then close the sale, or determine if the prospect qualifies for a field-sales visit. Telemarketing results can be enhanced by using other media or resources, in this example using direct mail and outside-sales personnel.

Brainstorm

The solution to your campaign's problems may come from your reps. Hold a brainstorming session with them. Write down everybody's ideas. Ask the group to suggest various novel approaches to solve the problem.

Is Telemarketing the Answer?

If a promotion hasn't been successful using other marketing media, don't think telemarketing is the answer; something may be wrong with the promotion itself. Only after you fix the problem in the promotion should you try a telemarketing pilot.

Coaching

During a tough campaign, increase your coaching time with those reps who are performing marginally. Have your supervisors compile daily statistics about these reps. If a rep's performance falters, the supervisor should work one-on-one with the rep, focusing on problem areas, motivating with pep talks, and providing incentives for improvement. One center takes a more intense approach with low performers by compiling statistics hourly, and by doing immediate coaching. Sometimes no amount of coaching will work because the rep isn't suited to the job.

Solutions Board

Hang up a bulletin board in a prominent place in your center. Tell managers and supervisors to post file cards listing current problems. Provide blank file cards so employees can post their solutions to the problems. Award prizes for all workable solutions.

Consultants

Sometimes you can't seem to find the problem or fix the campaign. You may be too close to the problem, and you may need someone to take a fresh look. Obtain the services of a consultant to evaluate the situation. In his book *Telemarketing: Setting Up for Success*, Michael R. Burns suggests asking these questions when interviewing a prospective consultant.

- How long have you been a telemarketing consultant?
- How long have you been involved in telemarketing?

- What is your background? Work experience? Schooling?
- Have you been an actual caller or a telemarketer before? Where? What did you sell? What were your results?
- Have you been a telemarketing or phone-room supervisor before? Where? What were your duties?
- Which clients have you worked for as a consultant? What did you do for them? What were the results? May I call them for references?
- What are your fees?
- Are you familiar with sources of lists? Where might I get a list for my program?
- What would be a rough sample script for my program?
- Can you send me some literature, a proposal, and a contract?

9
CUSTOMER SERVICE

If you lose your focus on customers, you'll lose your competitive edge. Companies that provide outstanding customer service have a significant competitive advantage. Excellent service adds important value to a product line. The value of a satisfied customer is unlimited. It's no longer enough to offer only quality products. There has been a significant shift away from *price* and towards *service*. As products and services proliferate, companies must turn to exceptional service to distinguish themselves from their rivals. Today, world-class companies embrace a total-quality process; customer satisfaction is top priority. These companies are committed to total customer satisfaction, even if it means short-term losses.

Customer service is more than just a customer-service department, or merely a friendly rep. Quality service is an integral part of every activity in your center.

Goals set by companies should be based on customer requirements and expectations, rather than on internal company standards.

There will be an evolution in telemarketing closely intertwined with quality service. Become a leader of this evolution. Continually introduce new products and improve old products by finding ways to give them more value.

Those who actually deliver customer service must be the best—hired carefully, trained thoroughly, regularly retrained, and empowered to serve the customers' needs. Like those best-in-class companies that offer superior service, schedule weekly meetings with your reps, work groups, or departments.

As Tom Peters notes, there's no such thing as an insignificant improvement. He believes that small is very beautiful. He also says there needs to be constant stimulation. To avoid the doldrums as you implement quality procedures in your company, Peters says, "the antidote is new goals, new themes, new rewards, new team champions, new team configurations, and new celebratory events."

The following chapter is about creating a customer-focused culture in your center.

Evolution of the Marketing Process

During the 1960s, companies concentrated on marketing to achieve a competitive advantage. In the 1970s, the focus was on manufacturing. The 1980s brought the era of quality. The new era of customer service dawns, and the companies who build a reputation for good service will hold the lead and beat the competition.

Davidow and Uttal, coauthors of *Total Customer Service: The Ultimate Weapon*, say, "Most managers don't invest heavily in service because they can't see bottom-line effects." The authors believe that the "most obvious benefits of superior service, like those of total quality control, come in terms of money saved." Providing good customer service eliminates the heavy cost of alienating buyers.

The authors further suggest that the cost of landing a new customer is three to five times more expensive than the cost of retaining an old customer.

Era of Quality Service

Robert E. Allen, Chairman of AT&T, says that "quality is customer satisfaction." However, quality is not a short-term project and it involves more than telling employees to "think quality." A program for converting thought into action must be implemented.

Patrick L. Townsend, author of *Commit to Quality*, believes that there are two types of quality.

Quality in fact The definition of quality lies solely with the provider. The company performs up to its own specifications.

Quality in perception This is quality as the customer sees it. A product achieves quality when it meets customer expectations.

Townsend believes attention must be paid to both definitions for sustained success.

Townsend says that if a company advertises quality, it had better deliver it if it wants to keep its profits, because a disappointed customer doesn't buy twice. He suggests that

> producing an object that is physically perfect does not solve the problems of quality for a paper-and-ideas industry. Convenience, promptness, courtesy, reliability, and other "soft" measurements more often serve as criteria for determining a quality service company.

These are measurements you can control in your center.

Delivering a consistently excellent service means hard work. Quality service is a "fix," but it's almost always a "slow fix." Research indicates that companies providing superb service have two things in common: a good service idea and a willingness to work incredibly hard to make the idea work.

The experts tell us that quality, customer satisfaction, and excellence in service are not easy to achieve, but that they're necessities in today's marketing environment. Steven Gentry, director of Milliken (a textile firm), and winner of the 1989 Malcolm Baldrige National Quality Award, states, "Quality by the book just won't work. You have to make it yours, you have to adapt it to your company culture. Even little changes like words and titles can make a difference." Milliken's company policy encourages anyone to change almost anything if it's an improvement. This "opportunity for improvement" program is so popular that each Milliken "associate" (employee) submits an average of nineteen suggestions per year. Think of the impact on your center if you received just one usable idea from each of your reps just once a year.

Organize for Service Improvement

Zeithaml, Parasuraman, and Berry wrote in their book *Delivering Quality Service* that successful organizational efforts for service improvements suggest the following principles, presented here in an abbreviated format.

- Create service-improvement roles. For service improvement to have a chance, it has to become part of your staff's main responsibilities. Create formal and informal organizational roles. Formal roles might include membership in service-improvement groups. Informal roles could involve being a "service defender" or "service champion."
- Create an integrative mechanism. Create a high-level interdepartmental steering group to energize, manage, and coordinate service-improvement efforts. This group generates, evaluates, and recommends service-improvement ideas. This group brings cohesiveness to the process.
- Develop a statement of direction. One of the steering group's main functions is to determine what needs to be done to improve service. This involves a realistic assessment of the present and a definition of what's needed in the future.

The authors suggest that "to get started in service improvement, prepare a succinct, written statement of direction that can be a continuing guideline for the service-related decisions that follow." The document should be strategic rather than tactical, long-term in focus rather than short-term, and grounded in empirical assessment rather than based on a few people's assumptions.

- Involve many and emphasize teamwork. Get as many people involved as possible, and get them involved in teams. Involvement in a team is renewing, stimulating, invigorating. The team concept actually improves individual performance. To let down the boss is bad, but to let down the team is often worse. Using service-improvement teams is a potent motivator. One gains the recognition and respect of peers when one does well, and their disdain when one does poorly.

In organizations, people depend on one another to deliver excellent service. The service process normally involves a chain of related services and servers. Service quality is rarely the sole result of isolated individual action. Teams should meet and exchange information often. They need to celebrate victories, learn from defeats, receive recognition and reinforcement.

- Think evolution rather than revolution. The complexity and enormity of the service-quality challenge often inhibits management's willingness to act. The authors' remedy? Aim for steady improvement rather than breakthrough change. Improving service becomes a more inviting challenge, a more practical endeavor when one breaks big problems into little problems and seeks continuous improvement. For example, simplifying an inbound script can result in a customer's clearer understanding of your products' features and benefits. Simplifying the script can cut talk time, too.

What Is Customer Service?

Is customer service as simple as a smile, a thank-you, or cheerful small talk after a negotiation? It begins there, but the opportunities for serving customers are endless. Begin by thinking of all the activities that could increase your customers' enjoyment of your product.

Identify the areas where customers might need help, and then tell customers that you're ready to provide them with that help. Customer service, according to the *Shaw MacLeod Telemarketing Report*, also comes in the form of "guarantees, warranties, training in product usage, technical advice, suggestions for alternate-product use, product-user clubs, follow-up customer contact, and company newsletters." You can generate revenue with customer service "through the sale of maintenance contracts, extended warranties, and even membership fees from user clubs."

Becoming Customer-Focused

According to the Forum Corporation, there are six key imperatives to creating customer focus.

- Build commitment to customer focus.
- Get in touch with customers.
- Build customer-focus teams.
- Break down barriers for the customer.
- Measure and report progress.
- Keep the process going.

Create a Customer-Service Culture

Deal with the customer to the customer's perception of service standards, not your own. A company without customer focus is guilty of short-term thinking. Customer service must be a team effort, including all the departments in the company, not just customer-interface groups.

Customer education is mandatory, whether it's in the scripts you write, or in the literature you send out. Once a customer understands how your company works, service problems begin to decrease.

Your goal in customer service is not just to excel, but also to make a profit and to increase your market share. Don't focus on what customer service costs, but on what it returns to your company. Eliminate any service features that customers don't want; they may be costing you more than they're worth.

Continually monitor the procedures, personnel, and systems in your center. Regularly measure your performance against your center's standards, and take corrective action before any substantial damage is done to your relationships with your customers. Stay in the lead, and be sure that customers can see the difference between you and your competitors.

Start a group where employees can share their experiences, the methods they use to handle customers, and how they provide quality service. From the group's description of how it helps customers, create a list of customer-service standards for reps to follow. Let your reps help set the standards.

Are complaints getting to the right departments? Create processes to ensure that they do. Set up an ongoing "managers' roundtable" where reps can talk directly to managers regarding the complaints they hear from customers. By listening carefully to potential or current customers, new uses for products can be found. Customers can also suggest new products and new service ideas.

Customers want convenience and value when they order a product or when they ask about a service. Decide whether your company should use a toll-free 800 number.

Assess Your Need for a Customer–Service Telemarketing Program

Depending upon the nature of your business, customer service can involve questions about repair, replacement, maintenance, service, delivery, shipping, billing, and more. First look at how your company now handles customer service. Ask yourself these questions: How do I process customer inquiries (calls or letters) now? Do most of my unsolicited calls and letters concern complaints, repairs, or suggestions?

What are my primary customer-service objectives? Answering shipping/inventory/billing questions? Handling complaints? Reducing repair calls? Educating consumers? Improving the company image? Earning customer loyalty? Which customer services should I provide, and why? Which customer groups am I most interested in reaching? In which geographic area?

Who currently determines how to best handle complaints, and who should handle them? How long does it take to resolve a customer's service request? How many of my employees handle a typical customer-service request? If I use salespeople to handle customer service, does this cut down the time they could be selling? Won't this cost me new sales? Is it possible that I'm losing customers to the competition because my customer-service department takes too long to come up with answers?

Customer–Service Reports

The aim of the reports generated by your customer-service department should be to solve problems. Don't categorize complaints and inquiries in a way that has meaning only for your own group. These reports should help other department managers who have the authority to fix problems. Communicating concerns immediately to the proper people can help solve and prevent complaints in the future. The customer-service department should avoid handling problems; it should report them to individual employees for action, instead. Customer inquiries should be reported back to the appropriate groups; these inquiries may indicate a need for rep training or customer education.

Keep Close to Your Customers

Keep your name in your customers' minds and listen to what they say. Call customers to offer them your services. Offer toll-free 800 numbers, and help-lines. If you're about to do a customer-satisfaction telephone survey, send customers a letter, or the survey itself beforehand. After you've made a sale, send a personalized thank-you letter to your customer. Send an apology letter after you've solved a customer's problem. Keep in touch with customers by sending out informational newsletters or brochures.

Create a "find information" center. When your reps receive calls from prospects and the reps aren't certain where to send the callers, transfer the call to this hotline. The experts there can solve the problem immediately, or, while still on the line, they can direct the prospect to the proper department. Set up an exclusive hotline for those customers who don't require field-sales visits but who still require individual attention. Informal customer feedback is valuable. Be sure to record compliments as well as complaints, and customers' ideas. Develop an "our customer says" form to record this information. Hold regular focus groups with your customers. Include postpaid customer comment cards when you ship your products. Form customer user-groups.

Measure the Performance of Your Customer-Service Program

Regularly monitor the performance of your customer-service program through customer-satisfaction tracking systems—number and types of complaints and compliments—and through in-house quality reviews.

Do "check" calls by calling your center to determine the kind of treatment given to prospects. Third-party vendors can also do this for you.

Call customers back a few days after a transaction to get their feedback about your reps.

Measure the Customer's Perception of Your Service

Ron Zemke, editor of the *Service Edge*, suggests reviewing the following ten steps to determine how customers perceive your service.

- Begin with your service strategy. Which promises and which measurements are implied in your service strategy? If you promise 24-hour turnaround on orders and zero defects, you can measure the turnaround time internally, but tracking defects involves communicating with your customers. When service falls short of expectations, where do the breakdowns occur? What happens to the customer?
- Measure frequently. Measure at least monthly, so information is fresh.

- Ask customer-based questions that are fair. Ask customers not only what happened during their transaction with your company, but how they felt about it. Be specific, and ask about things that your people can act upon.
- Collect group and individual data.
- Collect information at least three times a year regarding your competitors' sales, market share, and customer satisfaction.
- Collect quantitative and qualitative data. Collect numerical ratings (on a scale of 10, customers say we rate . . .) and specific customer comments.
- Make the results visible. Display the results of your measurements to emphasize their importance, and to actively involve frontline employees in the process.
- Make the results employee-friendly. Simple, straightforward numbers work best. Some people are more comfortable knowing that "87% of all customers said . . ." or "nearly nine out of ten customers surveyed feel . . ." than they are trying to understand the statistical significance of medians or weighted averages.
- Make the results believable. Don't pass down information from the top of your organization after some outside firm has conducted surveys and expect your employees to believe it. Involve employees in the process, or at least make them aware of how the information is gathered and assure them that it comes from their customers, and they'll be likely to act on it.
- Use the results. It isn't enough to send out a memo listing results or complaints compiled in a customer survey. Discuss the survey widely. Use the results as the basis for problem-solving meetings and to celebrate successes, and your staff will regard the information as important.

Fix the Inside First

Zemke and Bell, authors of *Service Wisdom*, believe that companies can create a favorable environment for customer service by treating customer-contact personnel both as employees and as "partial customers" who deserve the same courteous treatment that you'd want your customers to receive. They view employees as internal customers, even going so far as to use survey research and market-segmentation strategies to offer employees customized jobs and flexible hours. They believe that when service employees feel that the company meets their needs, they then feel free to concentrate on meeting customer needs.

Davidow and Uttal rightly note that "customer relations mirror employee relations." They offer additional suggestions on how to create a positive climate for customer service and how to treat your frontline employees. Demonstrate concern for employees, enhance their dignity, solve their problems quickly and fairly, and exalt their importance. Institute a range of human-resource policies that employees view favorably. Show respect for employees, and show each employee that you think he's competent.

Customer service begins on the inside. Employees should respond to coworkers with the same zeal that's required to exceed customer expectations.

Train the Frontline

The training program for customer-service reps should match the reality of what's actually happening in the center, and not what policies *say* should be happening. Maintain a close relationship between training and operations, so that when reps enter the "real" world after training, they won't perceive a difference.

Customer Service Is Everybody's Business

Everyone in the company is involved in customer service, from the employee who designed the brochures to the person who balances the budget. Everyone must send a positive and service-oriented message to the customer. It's the center manager's responsibility to show employees how their jobs fit in with the goals of the company.

Townsend says that the "key to the motivation of every employee and the first step in involving everyone in attaining quality is to give every employee well-defined customers." He believes that by expanding the definition of customer, the concept of quality and the contributions possible from each person become much clearer. The customer isn't just the person who buys your products and services, he's anyone to whom your employees provide any information, product, or service. Your employee's primary customer may be the person at the next desk.

Davidow and Uttal believe that "there are few quicker ways to improve service than to make everyone in your company responsible for it—no matter what department he or she is in." This doesn't mean that companies should do away with their customer-service departments. These departments are still needed as a point of contact for customers. What the authors propose is to expand the concept of customer service from that of a special department, particular person, or customer-service desk to the concept of customer service as an integral part of work life.

The Rep's Role in Customer Service

Get your reps involved in determining the areas that need improvement. Reps may identify some barriers you weren't even aware of. Challenge them to come up with innovative solutions that will promote excellent service in your company. Let them take risks; take the time to explore options with them.

Implement a "charm your customer" campaign. Instead of telling reps how to do it, ask them what they do to make their customers happy. Give awards based on effort, originality, and personalized service.

Hold a "focus on the customer" workshop. Hold an informal session with reps where you post customer expectations on a large easel. During the week, display this list prominently.

At your next weekly meeting, create two more lists. Post the items that your center really does well. Next, list those things that need to be improved. Post these lists in the center, too. A week later hold your last session. Let the group come up with solutions to the areas needing improvement that were discussed the week before. You may want to schedule these workshops every three months.

When you find an error in an order, tell the rep who made the mistake to call or write the customer. If a letter is sent to the customer, let the rep sign it. The employee involved will understand the importance of doing his job well.

Opportunities from Customer Complaints

Linda M. Lash, author of *The Complete Guide to Customer Service*, believes that

> complaints and inquiries provide the opportunity to educate customers, to cement brand loyalty, to turn negative word-of-mouth advertising into positive word-of-mouth advertising, in fact, to make a profit from perceived service failures.

Listening to customers can also tell you which products you need to develop in the future.

One large company handles over three million consumer inquiries a year, with a satisfaction level of over 90%. It does this all in the name of customer service. The center manager claims that the purpose of the center "is to offer the same personalized service many small businesses do."

What puzzles the manager is why companies don't take customer complaints more seriously. He says,

> Most of [the companies] don't understand that inquiry-handling is an opportunity to build loyalty and to get sales. Many companies think that if they hide from complaints that they will go away. Well, they won't. Those with problems left unanswered will go to the competition.

He adds, "Customer service is really selling." This successful center produces at least twice the return its company originally expected. The company spends between $2.50 and $4.50 on a typical call, and reaps two to three times that amount in additional sales and savings from unused warranty repairs.

Progressing from complainants to loyal customers is a complex process. Linda M. Lash suggests that managers should be cautious when measuring customer complaints. The number of complaints doesn't measure the level of service provided by a company, but only measures how many customers complained. The success of a customer-service center depends upon the service given that causes customers both to spread positive word-of-mouth advertising and to purchase a product again. Powell Taylor's experience confirms this. Only 10–15% of the GE center's calls are complaints, but these complaints are welcomed. "We want complaints to surface," says Taylor, "because research shows that only 4% of dissatisfied customers complain. The rest say nothing to you, but plenty to their friends and family. If you can satisfy the complainers, 80% of them rebuy."

Customer Confrontations

How many times have you said to yourself "If it hadn't been for that problem customer, my day would have been easier"? In quieter moments, admit that there are no problem customers, just customers with problems. Their displeasure probably arose from some oversight caused by your company. Rather than labelling these people as "impossible" or "hypercritical," train your reps to concentrate on the issues, listen to customers' concerns without trying to define them, and then to take action to find the right solutions.

Tips for handling customer confrontations

- Never argue with a customer; this makes the situation worse.
- Allow the customer to vent his feelings.
- Take notes, writing down the key points that will help you solve the problem.
- Remain polite and calm.
- Ask the customer to describe the facts; this should help you to separate the facts from emotions.
- Remember to deal only with the facts.
- Stay firm.
- Cater to your customer's sense of fair play, telling him you want to do what's right. Imply that you think of him as a person of integrity. This may nudge *him* to do what's right.
- Empathize with the customer, offering some soothing remarks.
- Recommend a solution that you can immediately implement, or refer the customer to the proper person. Make sure that the customer indeed makes contact with that proper person.

Are you making your customers angry?

All you're doing is "doing your job." How can you be responsible for making customers angry? It *is* possible, according to Mary Beth Ingram, president of PhonePro. Ingram suggests that reps may set the tone for an angry response without realizing it. She says of handling difficult phone calls, "We telegraph what we feel in our voices." Ingram offers a remedy:

> Ask yourself these four questions about your voice pattern on any given phone call. A "yes" answer to any of the questions may signal that you're giving the green light to a caller to go right ahead with a tirade, regardless of what you're saying: 1. Does my voice sound tired? 2. Does my voice sound interrupted? 3. Is my voice rough and gruff? 4. Is my voice timid and shy?

Ingram believes that we should take the attitude that every call is going to be a positive experience. Try conveying this "can-do" attitude the next time you pick up the phone. You'll like the results.

The Cost of Complaints

The concept of quality is important in every department of your organization. High-volume, low-quality sales will cost you more than low-volume, high-quality sales. Ensure the quality of your sales by calling back to verify the orders. Do this randomly, or for every sale. Monitor your reps on an ongoing basis.

If a customer disputes a charge of $5–10, it might be better to absorb the charge than to risk losing the customer. You may gain a loyal customer.

Track complaints regularly, by department or by division, and then analyze the cost of solving each complaint (employees' time, phone calls, research). An increase in quality-control procedures should result in a decrease in complaints and a financial savings.

Win and Keep Customers

You can win and keep customers by using the following tips.

- The only two things customers buy are good feelings and solutions to problems.
- Rewarding the customer is everybody's business.
- To win new customers, ask: "What's the unmet want?"
- Whenever you have a contact with a prospect, *you* are the company to that person.
- Help the customer buy what's best for him.
- How customers are treated reflects how management treats its employees.
- If your service quality is poor, ask yourself what's being rewarded. Do you reward your employees for something other than taking care of your customers?
- Solicit service-improvement ideas from everyone.
- Walk around your center and see what's going on.
- Make heroes of your frontline workers by training, motivating, and promoting them.

The Lifetime Value of Your Customer

Marketing has evolved from focusing on the simple acquisition of a customer, to repeat sales; its new goal is the lifetime value of the customer. Accurate calculation of lifetime value is no easy task. No matter which method you use, determining the lifetime value of a customer is critical. Ernan Roman, author of *Integrated Direct Marketing*, says,

For virtually all sellers of goods and services, it is repeat business over time that not only provides the bulk of the profit but also brings in new customers through referrals.

Marketing to current customers is also more profitable than marketing to new prospects.

Lost Customers

Before you search for new prospects, consider remarketing to your "lost" customers, those who haven't purchased from your company within the last year. Find these "lost" customers in your data base, or in your "no sale" reports. Send them a warm, friendly letter indicating that you've missed serving them. Tell them that you'll be calling soon to determine how you can best meet their needs.

Whenever you lose a customer, ask yourself what you did to lose him. What can you do to win him back? Develop a plan to avoid losing current customers. Initiate a formal, ongoing "win-back" program to bring back those lost customers.

Reps—the Company's Image

Many times, your company's image is your rep's voice. Since the only contact a customer may have with your company may be with your reps, your rep *is* the company to your customer. You're only as good as your reps, since their service is the company's product.

Rating Customer-Service Reps

Your reps' skills and motivation usually determine their sales for the month. "X" number of sales equals "X" reward. Rating customer-service reps is trickier. How do you rate "service"? Customer-service reps at one telemarketing center have designed an innovative incentive program for themselves called "Employee of the Month." This program rates each rep each month on one of several customer-service criteria.

- Rep who handles the most incoming calls
- Rep who's shown the most improvement over a six-month period
- Best attendance/most punctual
- Best phone manner
- Best technical knowledge
- Most assistance to teammates

One of the above criteria is the focus of each month's award, but reps don't know from month to month which particular measure is being judged for that month. The monthly award consists of a small trophy and a paid day off. The winner's name is engraved on a plaque that's displayed in the department. A unique feature of this incentive program is a cumulative-point system which enables any member of the department to know exactly how he's rated on a specific measure. Reps can also qualify for an "Employee of the Year" award. The award consists of a paid day off and dinner with the company's vice president.

The program is regularly reviewed by a rep task force to determine if any changes or improvements are needed.

Increase Customer Satisfaction by Managing It!

William A. Band, in an article entitled "Creating a Customer Focused Organization," claims that companies can increase customer satisfaction through the management of five factors.

- Products, or services, properly designed from a user's point of view
- Careful presale communication that creates realistic expectations of product performance
- After-sales support to ensure that products deliver their promised benefits while in use
- Feedback which encourages quick response to changing customer needs
- Emphasis on customer satisfaction as the driving force of the organization

Close the Customer "Loop"

If you send a letter to a customer saying that you'll be calling him soon, but you never do, send another letter stating that you tried to contact him, but that he wasn't at home. Then go into the reason for your call. Sending the second detailed letter will assure that the customer received the important information.

Encourage Customer Feedback

Provide an incentive for customer feedback. Each time a customer fills out a service evaluation form, enter his name into a sweepstakes.

"A Day in the Life"

Implement "A Day in the Life" training program. Employees try out other jobs to understand the various roles other employees fill.

Visible Management

Have senior executives and middle managers work in frontline service-delivery positions, where they have direct contact with customers and other employees. Managers will get a realistic impression of the challenges faced by reps. They'll also be able to verify data obtained from other management sources, and they'll hear customers' concerns firsthand.

Reps also benefit from "visible management." They have the opportunity to speak with managers, and the reps will be able to express their opinions and ideas in their own familiar environment.

Twelve Ways to Keep Customers

- Use toll-free 800 numbers.
- Follow up with callbacks after a service concern has been resolved.
- Include comment cards with merchandise.
- Send letters of recognition to loyal customers.
- Assign reps whose sole responsibility is your top accounts.
- Invest in relationship-building by spending more time on your customers.
- Think of yourself as the customer. What would your needs be?
- Reward loyal customers with discounts.
- Implement formal customer-complaint procedures. Some centers resolve complaints in forty-eight hours.
- Reward reps for providing customers with superior service.
- Offer satisfaction guarantees.
- Always solicit customer feedback.

Easy to Do Business With

In 1986, AT&T introduced a program called "Easy to Do Business With," to enable employees to provide quality service to customers. All reps follow specific procedures during a telemarketing call, when a customer asks a question or seeks help with a problem not related to the product the reps are selling. The rep must either resolve the issue, direct the customer to the appropriate office, or complete the necessary paperwork and then send it to the appropriate office.

The Trick to Customer Service

The *Service Edge* newsletter suggests six simple steps to better customer service. Originally developed for employees who work face-to-face with customers, these steps have been adapted for reps who deal with phone customers.

- Greet customers.
- Value customers.
- Ask how to help customers.
- Listen to customers.
- Help customers.
- Invite customers back.

Doing each step in sequence ensures success.

Business Customer-Service Checklist

Do you offer value-added services to your business customers? These services will give you a competitive edge. Provide and emphasize those benefits that are important to maintain your customers' interest and their business.

- Keep customers aware of all your new products and services.
- Call customers at regular intervals. The specific calling schedule should depend upon the level of business you have with them.
- Keep customers aware of important price, personnel, and policy changes.
- Think of ways to help customers improve their business by promoting the products and services that will help them in the marketplace. First analyze the way their business works, and then suggest improvements.
- Suggest a new promotion, or innovative ways to sell or serve their own customers differently. Know your customers' business.

Cultivate the Customer Contact

Lash talks about the "inverted pyramid" in customer service. Turn the organization upside down, and put the decision-making power into the hands of the frontline employees. Reps will have the authority to select a course of action to satisfy customers. This strategy encourages employees to think, and to use their own judgment, within the framework of the company's service goals.

Experience shows that the benefits of "frontline empowerment" include a low number of complaints received in the customer-service department, and at headquarters. The less time it takes to resolve a complaint, the less costly it is for the company, and the less chance for negative word-of-mouth advertising. Putting the power in your reps' hands can supplement expensive market research and customer surveys. The rep has the power to choose an action plan that will satisfy customers.

Encourage your reps to cultivate customer contacts. They should keep a plan of action in mind before talking to customers. If there's an unhappy customer on the line, what information do they and your company need to help solve the problem?

To maintain that competitive edge, coach reps to strive for excellence in each customer contact. Remind reps that each customer expects courtesy and prompt attention. Each customer contact is a sales call, and these calls can result in more, or less, business.

Reps should use these two ways to identify customer expectations.

- Ask
- Listen

Encourage good communication skills. Make it a practice to attempt to solve customer complaints as they arise.

Eight Action Steps for Improved Customer Satisfaction

John A. Goodman, President of Technical Assistance Research Programs (TARP), offers the following eight steps.

- Quantify where you are. Quantify the level of problems and market damage so that you can estimate the benefits that will come from improvements and set specific targets. If you don't quantify, you'll never justify the investment needed to improve your product.

- Set targets for improvement and link them to rewards.
- Train and empower your frontline service and marketing staff to solve problems.
- Solicit complaints via 800 numbers. Encourage customers to resolve complaints at a local retail outlet first.
- Automate your service and quality-control systems to record and analyze the causes of complaints. By collecting, collating, and reporting this data, action plans will be quickly achieved.
- Create a focal point for customer satisfaction and prevention of future problems.
- Invest in customer education. Look for opportunities to educate customers when you write your scripts, and when you mail your literature.
- Keep track of satisfaction by analyzing individual transactions.

Goodman believes that you should keep four things in mind if you're to be successful in customer satisfaction.

- Quantify where you are, and where you're going.
- Look at your internal systems.
- Listen to your customers to determine the causes of their dissatisfaction.
- Measure and reward tangible decreases in customer problems.

To ensure that your customer-service center is also a profit center, Goodman and Grimm say that you must achieve two main goals.

- Resolve problems rapidly to promote increased loyalty and increased sales.
- Generate additional sales from calls only after the basic problem or question has been handled.

However, Goodman warns that the ability of the customer-service center to be a corporate profit center depends upon its effectiveness. If the center can't effectively handle individual customer contacts, and use the data that it gathers to eliminate the root cause of problems, it may be better for the company not to solicit such contacts at all.

The TARP formula for customer satisfaction states, "Do the job right the first time. Add effective customer contact management to equal maximum customer loyalty."

Enhance Customer Service with 800 Numbers

Such numbers can help your company identify and reach customers who have questions and problems. TARP research demonstrates that "customers who have questions but who don't request assistance would contact the company if there were a readily accessible 800 number."

You can retain customers by using 800 numbers. Research by TARP indicates that a "customer-service 800 number is more effective than a correspondence-based system in maximizing customer loyalty." The key factor in customer satisfaction (how their requests for help are handled) is the timeliness of the response. An immediate response can often be provided by an 800 number.

Customer-service costs can be decreased by using 800 numbers. Studies show customer-contact reps need less time to respond to a phone contact than they do to a request submitted by mail. Customers associate 800 numbers with quality products and services.

Toll-free numbers enable companies to gather data about customers' problems. These data serve as early-warning flags. Companies can take immediate action to correct problems. Customers can be questioned at length, enabling the company to identify the problem.

An 800 number provides a tool for determining customers' needs. Once you've determined these needs, your company can develop new products and it can determine the success or failure of current products.

The 800 number is also a handy tool for customer education. You can instruct consumers about proper product use. A customer's improper use of a product can lead to dissatisfaction and reduced loyalty.

Customer Education

Educating the customer from the start increases customer satisfaction and increases your company's success. Educate customers, and you'll help your reps deliver superior service. When reps have to repeat the same instructions over and over, or when customers are confused by product directions and literature, you demoralize your reps and tarnish your company's reputation.

TARP has discovered that "40% of customer dissatisfaction is a result of the customer not being adequately educated on how to get proper performance from the product." Goodman says, "If the customer is educated on how to use the product, he will not make as many mistakes and will not contact the company with problems or questions due to improper use or incorrect expectations." Companies are now aware that "preventive education" costs less than solving problems after the damage is done.

Use Teams to Solve Service Problems

When you have a specific service challenge, form a team of employees to work on the issue. The team approach contributes to superior service delivery, and is noticed by customers. Work with the team to create a primary goal and to develop a service strategy to solve the problem. When assessing the task, ask these questions: Does the work do what it's intended to do? Is there a better way of doing it? Is it repetitious? Is it outdated?

Fifty Tips for Improving Customer Service

- Act upon survey results; don't just collect data.
- Input the customer's name/address change in your data base immediately after it's given to you.
- Help customers purchase what's best for them.
- Identify which service-improvement ideas you can implement now.
- Treat customers as partners-for-life.
- Don't jump to conclusions about what your customers are thinking; you could be focusing on the negative.
- Lower your voice when a customer yells at you. The customer may lower his voice, too.
- Ask customers how they rate your company's customer service. Ask them what they'd like improved.
- Develop procedures for "handoffs" (sending a complaint to another department, e.g.). Inform the customer of the "handoff." Fill out a customer-service complaint/inquiry form. Jointly develop the "handoff" procedures, in advance, with the departments involved. These procedures should designate which department completes the transaction.
- Establish your company as a service organization and as an authority on products. Offer customers advice before they purchase your products.
- Put apologies in the first person, using "I." "We" is impersonal.
- When dealing with irate customers, be aware of your tone of voice; keep it sincere and helpful. Banish sarcasm and anger. Keep the pitch of your voice level, and monitor its volume. Don't let your voice rise, or disappear into a whisper.
- Remember that each contact with a customer must be first-time fresh.
- Begin your calls with a strong, warm responsive introduction to put you in control of the dialogue.
- Improve your listening skills by paraphrasing your customer's remarks. Summarize a point back to the customer to check understanding, and to seek feedback.
- Listen to the customer's concerns without trying to define them.
- Remember that your company should experience the variables in service, not the customers. For example, employees' lunch breaks shouldn't be scheduled at the same time as the customers', because calls won't get through.
- Listen to what the customer hears.
- Win and keep customers by rewarding them.
- Make follow-up service calls, even if the customer was angry during his last call. If the customer still has problems, you can correct them. If the problem's solved, the customer will appreciate the call.
- Watch out for negative responses, such as, "We're out of that item." Offer a choice or an alternative. "We'll be getting those folders in next

month, but in the meantime, we have a good price on some other folders that you may be able to use."

- Agree with an angry customer. As soon as you agree, you'll appear to be working with him, instead of against him.
- Think of the customer in terms of his lifetime value.
- Sell customer service to upper management by quantifying the value of customer retention. It's always less expensive to keep customers than it is to find new ones.
- Develop a marketing strategy to win back former customers. Classify your former customers by market segments, and develop a marketing plan for each group.
- Don't just fix the product, fix the customer by properly educating him.
- Think of customer service as a theatre, not as a factory.
- Be reliable.
- Be enthusiastic.
- Satisfy your customers by the end of the day, or let them know when their problem will be solved.
- Keep in touch with customers. Don't let your only contact occur when you send a bill, or when you're selling something.
- Follow the "policy exception" rule. An employee should try to solve a customer's problem rather than follow standard company policy.
- Do it right the first time.
- Bestow a monthly "spirit" award to the employee who makes you glad to be working where you do.
- Interview current and prospective customers to find out what they like, and what they don't like, about your business. Look for market niches and competitive advantages.
- Strive for high quality. High quality means few mistakes, which in turn means low costs.
- Throw away the policy manual and do whatever it takes to solve a problem.
- Tell your customers what you're going to do with the results of your surveys. Demonstrate the positive results of your surveys by providing enhanced services. Tell customers that these enhancements resulted from a past survey to which they'd contributed.
- Educate customers about your products and services as you conduct a survey.
- Review your business accounts quarterly for overall customer satisfaction. If your company isn't up to par, initiate an action plan to bring satisfaction levels up. This action plan could include additional telephone surveys, field visits to clients, letters to customers, or a problem-solving session with customers.
- Turn your employees' motivation into action that benefits your customers.

- Forward your reps' questions about product quality to your quality-control section, and then respond to your reps.
- Reward the person who's done the best job supporting his "internal" customers.
- Inform your customer immediately if your company won't be able to meet an agreed-upon deadline.
- Be sure you're receiving complaints. If customers complain, you haven't lost them yet. You'll still be able to resolve the problem, and to build a strong relationship.
- Boast about the customer service you provide in your advertising, promotional literature, direct mail, corporate letterhead, business cards, package inserts, giveaways, and on your products.
- Carefully track all inquiries and complaints. Categorize by subject, by product, by customer segment, by model number, and by type of repair.
- Mail personalized letters to your top customers, letting them know that you're always available for consultation.
- Verify information with a customer by repeating and confirming; you'll avoid problems later.
- Compensate for the lack of visual contact during a telephone conversation by telling customers what you're going to do for them. "I'll check the inventory on that item right now."

10
INTEGRATED DIRECT MARKETING

In the 1970s, telemarketing was relatively new. It offered many benefits to businesses: low cost, one-on-one contact, flexibility, and easy measurement. Yet, telemarketing had to struggle to achieve its rightful place among the related marketing media. During this time, there was some integration of the various media. Only now can you use a sophisticated and synchronized approach that will have a powerful, unified effect on the marketplace.

A coordinated interrelationship among diverse marketing media enhances the one-on-one telemarketing contact, and thus your profits. If you treat people as individuals, through the intelligence of data-base marketing, they will respond. In business today, look to build relationships, not just one-time-sale contacts.

IDM is a sophisticated marketing concept. Although it may appear complex at first, if you work on small chunks, build slowly, take time to learn, test, step back, and analyze, you'll be on your way to successful IDM.

Definition

Ernan Roman, author of *Integrated Direct Marketing*, provides a concise definition of this technique:

Integrated direct marketing is the art and science of managing diverse marketing media as a cohesive whole. These interrelationships are catalysts for response. The resulting media synergy generates response rates higher than could ever be achieved by individual media efforts.

This technique pulls together all of your marketing approaches into one smooth flow of information aimed at your customer. Each part (direct mail, advertising, telemarketing) builds on the next.

The foundation of IDM is data-base marketing—the gathering of information that helps you determine your target market.

Integration Plan

According to Bencin,

All the management cooperation, sound conceptual planning, and careful goal-setting in the world will avail you nothing, however, if you try to implement the telemarketing program in a vacuum. To have an effective telemarketing program, it is absolutely necessary to integrate telemarketing into the overall sales, advertising, and marketing program of the entire organization.

161

Selecting a "market universe," for example, should be directed by your company's manager of marketing and sales, since they usually have the detailed knowledge of such a "universe." Mutual understanding of common benefits is essential. For instance, there may be inactive accounts or "low-ticket" buyers that are uneconomical to visit in person. A field salesperson might be delighted to turn over these accounts to telemarketing.

Bencin believes,

> Sales isn't the only area that needs to be integrated with telemarketing. Tie-ins with the data processing department are also beneficial. Computer analysis may show that a company or store has a great many customers in certain neighborhoods or that there are many psychographic groupings. This suggests it would be easy to contact the prospects via telephone.

Bencin suggests that analysis of the U.S. OMB's primary and secondary Standard Industrial Classification codes (SICs) can disclose likely areas for potential customers. The data-processing people can help you code your prospects by source, company size, product type, etc., as well as help to keep track of payment and reorder patterns.

The following example shows IDM in action in business-to-business contacts: An advertising message contains a toll-free 800 number offering more information about a product. When a potential customer calls the 800 number, a rep gathers information for the data base. A direct-mail piece is then sent to the customer. One to two weeks later, the rep calls the prospect to find out if the information arrived. The rep questions the prospect's eligibility to determine the level of interest. The "qualified" lead is then given over to the field-sales staff for follow-up, or to close the sale.

Magic of IDM

Roman says,

> There's the magic . . . of integrated direct marketing that one plus one yields more than two. When a mailing piece which might generate a 2% response on its own is supplemented by a toll-free 800 number ordering channel, we regularly see response rise by 50%. The additional media we bring to the mix add new ways for prospects to respond to the information already provided and new interactive channels of communication for delivering additional information.

Another reason for integration is to ensure that the prospect experiences one continuous sales process. Whenever you plan a campaign, incorporate a single selling process in all your advertising. Ask yourself what messages your customers receive from your various media.

IDM: A Data-Base Builder

IDM helps the manager build useful and profitable data bases. Establish multiple channels of communication with prospects through IDM, including mail responses, 800-number response, outbound telemarketing, or a field-sales visit all within the context of one campaign. Roman says that the "goal is to aggressively use this information resource by capturing the data as it is uncovered and analyzing it to uncover the trends and significant patterns it describes."

To begin your integrated campaign strategy, start with a clear campaign objective that includes advertising, direct mail, and telemarketing. Set objectives. Good objectives are measurable, achievable, and in writing. Are you selling products? How many do you plan to sell? Is your objective to generate sales leads? How many? Set up a meeting so that all of your key personnel can review the objectives together, and decide on a common area of agreement. Plan how you'll achieve the objectives as a team.

Communicate

Establish and maintain effective, ongoing communication between all key players. Weekly team meetings will identify any unfinished business that, if not caught in the early stages, could destroy your campaign. When a change is made in one aspect of the campaign, communicate this change to all team members, because the new procedure could adversely affect the other steps in the program. Without ongoing dialogue, your campaign could fail.

Data-Base Marketing

The quality of your data base is essential for direct-marketing success. Regularly maintain and add to your data base. Each campaign effort should supply you with valuable data. Ernan Roman says that "the underlying goal of data-base marketing—the variable we are trying to maximize—is relevance."

Build and use your data base

Before you begin to build your data base, analyze your center's needs. Talk with your other team members. Put your needs in writing; be very specific.

- Plan for the future. Plan for extra "buckets" to capture information that may be required in the future. Plan for additional analytical and cross-matching needs to accommodate future changes.
- Don't collect too much of the "wrong" data. The cost of maintaining, storing, and processing will rise, as will the potential for error.
- Determine if the data is important, or needed. If you can't act on the information you gather, then it isn't needed.
- Integrate your data base to let you measure performance by campaign, by sales territory, or by customer group.

- Use your data base for more than just simple inquiry and sales-lead generation. Make your data base *work*. Segment your market and determine market potential to help you write telemarketing messages that will bring in sales. Careful analysis can help you market to the best prospects.
- Keep customer records current so you don't lose track of valued past purchasers.
- Maintain as much relevant information as possible about each customer, so you'll be able to aim your new products and services at the right audience.
- Train, retrain, and remind your reps to gather the necessary information. You might track sales history, response history, attitudinal information, purchase patterns and timing, as well as other data that can enhance and build your system, or help you to create customer profiles.
- Keep your data base vital by facilitating ongoing, interactive communication with your customers.
- Increase your profits by identifying a customer segment that promises the best rate of return. Determine the number of contacts needed to maximize sales to that group.

Roman maintains that data-base marketing involves two stages.

- Gathering and categorizing information to provide meaningful, actionable characteristics for marketing decision-making.
- Analyzing this data to determine the patterns which are significant indicators of purchase behavior.

Take full advantage of the benefits of data-base marketing to effectively sell, cross-sell, and upsell to your present customers. Analyze your valuable data to help you plan new products and services for the future. Include customer service as part of your strategy to help you keep those customers after you get them.

Personalization

Roman states,

> The real focus of personalization is not the mechanics of production (that is, the ability to personalize a direct mailing with an individual's name) but the targeting of individuals to receive the offer. The more accurately a direct-response contact addresses the perceived needs of the individual who receives it, the greater the response rate.

Lists

Your prospect list can greatly influence the overall response rate of your campaign. If you aren't promoting to the right people, your campaign could fail. The better you define your market, the better your list selection will be.

- Don't select lists by price. A low-cost list can mean low quality.
- Keep a list vital with fresh names. How current is the list? When was it last revised?
- Select prospect lists that mirror your ideal customer.
- Look for responsiveness. Contact someone who's been responsive to direct mail or to telemarketing.
- Look for frequency. How often has the prospect responded to direct mail or to telemarketing? The more often a prospect has responded, the more likely it is that he'll respond in the future.
- Choose your list wisely. A list that works for direct mail won't always be the best list for telemarketing.
- The list should have the decision-makers' names. Having the names will save your rep the time it could take to find the right contact.
- How much other "qualifying" information does the list have? Type of business, annual company sales, number of employees, number of locations? Income, age, credit history (for consumers)?
- What is the average sale (number of units, dollar value) in the list?
- Choose a list that contains a sufficient number of names to offer potential business.
- Choose a list that your competitor also rents.
- What's the source of your list? The source can tell you much about what a person will respond to.
- Test several different lists during a campaign. Track the response from each list.
- What kind of offer did the prospects on the list respond to? A prospect will be most receptive to an offer that he responded to in the past.
- Nurture, maintain, and add to your list regularly. Your best list is your existing customer data base.

Promotions and Direct-Response Advertising

Promotions are incentives to try or purchase a product, such as cents-off coupons, limited-time discounts, contests, or sweepstakes.

A promotion is often delivered through a combination of direct-response advertising and other media, such as in-store displays or on-package offers. Promotions usually last for a limited and specific time, and apply to both consumer and business-to-business goods and services.

Direct-response advertising asks for a specific, immediate response from your market; catalogs are good examples. The response asked for may be an immediate purchase, or it may be for specific additional information such as a booklet on a complex product.

Plan your promotion

Consider your objectives and how your promotion will help you meet them. Each promotion is unique. The combination of product, service, offer, advertising, size of target market, and sometimes seasonality will determine the response rate.

If you have limited experience with promotions, test your telemarketing promotion against a small segment of your market before your campaign begins. Response rates from the test can be used to estimate what you might expect from the entire market. Always do a pilot before a new campaign.

A telemarketing promotion requires extensive planning

- Who are your customers and prospects?
- Which media can you use to reach them?
- What action do you wish your target market to take? Purchase? Inquiry? Trial? A product demonstration?
- What products or services will be included in the promotion? A series of products, or just one product?
- What role will the promotion play in the center's sales process? Will the rep be doing lead-generation or order-taking?
- What's the key benefit that will be promoted? A special price offer?
- Are there any secondary benefits?
- What image does the company want to project? Image drives the creative design of a direct-mail package or an ad. Define your image before you get into creative development.
- What fulfillment pieces will be needed?
- What response rate are you looking for? If the promotion involves a simple order, you want as high a response rate as possible. However, if you focus on generating leads, your copy should screen out simple information seekers and target serious prospects.

Which Media?

Direct-response ads can run in any medium: TV, radio, print, mail, or billboards. Make your media choices based on your budget and the market you're trying to reach.

Never assume that one medium is enough. Running the same promotion in different media helps reinforce your message, and builds more sales. Mix and match your selection of media to target all market segments, or to zero in on specific segments exclusively.

Send One Message

Develop one cohesive selling strategy for your different channels. When a direct-response promotion is used in conjunction with telemarketing, the basic message and the targeting of the promotion should relate to the sales process that will take place on the phone. If a customer reads one message in the ad (or direct-mail piece), and hears something quite different from the rep, he'll be confused, and your company will lose credibility. If your center's efforts are coordinated, the prospects will call about the ad, and your rep will refer to the ad in front of him. The script the rep reads will also closely relate to the promotion's strategy. The rep is able to address the benefits mentioned in the ad, and to answer customer questions.

Develop your direct-mail copy in conjunction with your telemarketing script. Don't use direct-mail copy, exactly as it is stated, in your scripts. This won't work, since telemarketing is a conversational medium. You *can* use the same "buzz words," to tie together the different parts of your campaign.

Always review all of your print copy to make sure that you aren't making it harder for your reps to sell; they shouldn't have to explain the points of your direct-mail piece to the customer. The prices and premiums offered in all media should always match, unless you intend to test several distinct offers. If you test different offers, tell your reps.

During classroom sessions about the new campaign, discuss the basic offer, the benefits to be stressed, and the promised follow-through. The more complex the selling operation, the more important it is that the reps' sales presentation be closely tied to the offers made.

Media Pave the Way for the Rep

Television and radio both build credibility and make it easy for reps to sell—consumers know about the products and services in advance. The inherent credibility of broadcast adds more credence to the sales pitch. Print can do the same when it's introduced before a sales call.

The best time to introduce direct mail depends upon the products and services offered. Complex products first need a phone call to introduce the idea; a direct-mail piece then details the offer. A subsequent phone call closes the sale. For less complex products, a direct-mail piece is sent, and an outbound call follows from one to two weeks later.

Benefits of Integrated Telemarketing

Richard L. Bencin believes that "when used in concert with other direct marketing channels, telemarketing yields much greater response effectiveness than the traditional channels—or even telemarketing—can by themselves alone." The use of the phone, plus direct mail, provide a greater return over direct mail alone.

Bencin says, "A telemarketing/direct mail combination can be used in several ways. Direct-response programs can be triggered by mass mailings and 800 numbers. Some organizations follow up inbound responses with outbound calls to increase overall close rates." Another tactic to use is the "more limited and specific targeting of direct-mail lists to allow outbound telephone follow-up to nonrespondents as well." All direct mail would be followed by outbound calls.

Bencin believes that both the number of catalog orders and the size of the orders are increased by the use of 800 numbers. There is also "a greater opportunity for cross-selling (selling related items) and upselling (selling more expensive and profitable items)." Bencin advises utilizing appropriately trained reps instead of mere order-takers; using the latter group can be a waste of sales opportunities.

Bencin suggests that in business-to-business catalog marketing, outbound calls should be done first to determine proper contacts and develop interest before mailing the catalogs. Follow-up outbound calls, closing the sales, complete the cycle. Special telephone-only discounts can be offered later via outbound calls, after new customers are developed.

Screening Questions

Ask prospects the right screening questions to enhance the value of each prospect's name for future marketing efforts.

Increase Telemarketing Sales

Help your reps increase sales.

- Leave your readers with something to do after they read the direct-mail piece so that they won't procrastinate. Prod them to act *now*. Mention a specific date rather than a time period. "Offer expires May 15," instead of "expires in ten days."
- Include a simple guarantee in your offer to generate confidence and to help overcome the customer's reluctance to order an unknown product by phone.
- Feature the 800 number in your cover letter, brochure, coupon, and on your business-reply card.
- Teach your reps to ask for the order.
- Use an 800 number to make it easy for the customer to respond.
- Provide clear, sequential ordering information in your direct mail, or in your catalog copy.
- Accent *benefits* in your copy.
- Be sure that your script is positive and that your rep is a friendly listener.
- To increase sales, print your 800 number on every page of your catalog.

Definitions

Control This is a proven ad or direct-mail package for which there are confirmed and successful results. This ad becomes the standard against which variations and improvements are continually tested. If a major difference is being tested, tell the reps of the change so that they can correctly handle the new test approach.

Compiled lists These are lists compiled from a number of different sources, including directories, phone books, car registrations, census data, and trade associations. These lists are usually taken from data bases containing millions of records.

Response lists These lists include those who've responded to some sort of offer. These prospects may have redeemed a coupon, called an 800 number, subscribed to a magazine, purchased from a catalog or through telemarketing. With response lists, you'll know which offer was promoted, what was purchased, the cost of the item, when and how often the prospects responded, and the source of the response itself.

Direct Mail

A direct-mail letter can be your primary sales vehicle. Studies show that packages with letters consistently outpull those without. Test a brochure sent by itself against a sales letter sent along with a brochure. Write a sales letter as if you were talking to just one person. Make each reader feel as if the letter were written just for him.

Ask yourself these questions before you start writing direct-mail letters.

- What am I selling?
- To whom am I selling?
- Why should customers buy?

Make a strong business-to-business offer and increase responses by adding "Bill me" as a payment option. Accept credit-card orders on toll-free 800 numbers. Add a premium as an incentive for prompt or early payment. Allow the customer to keep the premium even if he returns the product.

Make your business-to-business telemarketing work for you. A call before the direct mail arrives alerts the prospect, generates anticipation, and gets the prospect to open the mail immediately. A follow-up call, after direct mail, can answer any of the prospect's questions. Make your follow-up calls from seven to ten days after the mailing.

Direct-Response Television

- Always look for opportunities to cross-sell and to upsell.
- TV commercials are usually 60, 90, or even 120 seconds long. Reserve 15 to 20 seconds to show and state your toll-free number early in the spot, and to repeat it again, with ordering instructions, later.
- Obtain immediate feedback on the response rate of a given outlet. In the case of broadcast, do this on a daily basis, tracking when and where the TV spots ran, and how they're performing.

- Target future advertising. To do this, Bencin suggests analyzing these variables: response percentage, day of week, time of day, time of response, linkage of response to spot, and length of spot. Using unique 800 numbers can help you quickly track response by TV station within specific markets.

Promote Team Spirit

Promote team spirit. Invite reps to appear in TV commercials, print ads, and brochures. Allow reps to participate in press interviews and to take special visitors on tours of the center.

Catalogs

Your reps should go beyond order-taking. Encourage them to probe actively for unexpressed customer needs that can be converted into upgrades and cross-sells.

Use techniques that stimulate sales. These include two-for-one offers, toll-free phone numbers, gifts to customers for placing an order, gift wrapping, an insert sheet in the catalog with last-minute specials, volume discounts for large orders, free pickup for returns, a thank-you note included with the order, free shipping and handling if orders are paid by check or money order, and allowing credit-card orders.

Test Different Vehicles

Regularly test direct-response advertising and promotions in different vehicles: magazines, newspapers, radio, television, catalogs, and direct mail. Carefully track which vehicle gives you the best response, highest number of sales, and the best cost per sale.

Make It Customer–Easy

In any direct-response ad, offer your customers a choice of ways to respond: a toll-free number, or a reply card. Most buyers will call the 800 number, but don't jeopardize sales by denying them a choice.

The easier you make it for a customer to respond, the more responses you'll receive.

Fulfillment Literature

In many telemarketing operations, literature is regularly sent to prospects describing the firm's products and services. When you create a new fulfillment brochure, let your reps review the art and the copy. Ask them if the copy adequately educates the prospect about your products and services. Are there paragraphs that confuse the prospect and contribute to unnecessary inbound calls? Does the copy support the firm's overall selling strategy?

Before You Mail That Literature

Before you send out literature that a prospect requests, ask yourself these questions.

- Does the brochure contain value-added information that would be too difficult for a rep to easily convey on the phone?
- Is the customer genuinely interested in reading the literature? Is he postponing a decision, or is he just easily terminating the call?
- Who will do follow-up with the prospect? Has a callback, with a specific date, been arranged?
- If it's the field staff's responsibility to follow up, have they been briefed on the current telemarketing campaign? Are they given properly qualified leads?
- Will the field-sales staff have a history of earlier customer/rep transactions so that they're aware of the prospect's knowledge of the products? Will they have customer profiles drawn from the center's data base?

After you send literature to a prospect, work out an action plan for each brochure you send out. Will the customer be contacted by the rep, by your field-sales staff, or by another direct-mail piece?

Measure Your Advertising Media's Effective Life

All advertising media have a measurable "effective life," ranging from the short life of a direct-mail piece to the longer life of a catalog. The effective life of the media used will directly affect the volume of response. Estimating inquiry volume is important, because volume substantially affects production requirements and total costs.

Estimate Response Volume

Adequately estimating the response usually comes with experience. Carefully compare the results of one campaign to another, taking all variables into consideration.

Direct mail

To increase 800-number response, the number should appear within the first two paragraphs of the letter, again in the body copy, and again in the postscript. Include the number several times in the brochure, and display it prominently on the order form or on the business-reply card.

Radio spots

Radio spots should repeat the 800 number and ordering information several times. Since a radio audience is likely to be without pencil and paper, easy recall is crucial. Group the last four numbers together (e.g., 1-800-555-4546). Advertise a "vanity" 800 number that spells something memorable. Studies show that the highest 800-number response rates occur when both the alpha and numeric forms are used in advertising.

Average Volumes

TV	TV spots will produce most calls within minutes of airing the commercial.
Print	Print will generate response over several days or weeks.
Direct Mail	Response will generally peak in a week or two.
Catalogs	Response continues for as long as several months.

If you mail to a large list, stagger your mailings to help even out responses.

Make the Most of Your 800 Numbers

To promote the use of an 800 number, many companies incorporate an easy-to-remember word or phrase in their number. Critics believe that although vanity numbers are easy to remember, they're sometimes difficult to dial. Proponents believe that prospects are more likely to remember a catchy number, rather than a word.

Measure, Track, and Test

Wise marketers regularly measure, track, and test response rates for all campaigns. Each new campaign offers a valuable learning experience that can only improve future programs.

If you mail a new promotion to a list of 5,000 or more, limit your risk by testing it on a small market segment first—at least 10% of the total.

Don't just count how many calls and reply cards came in; study where the best responses came from.

Compare different media, lists, offers, copy and design, and time of year to determine which combinations work best. When possible, test a new campaign against a "control"—one that worked well previously, in the same market. Analyze the response to your direct-mail and trade ads. Which is the most profitable?

Design your campaign so that it's easy to compare results later. If you mail to two different lists, or advertise in two different newspapers, give each channel its own phone extension to call, and code your mail-in coupons with the phone extension, too.

Establish systems to track all pertinent data concerning phone and mail response. Compare your spring and summer catalog sales. Track multiple mailings to see if they produce enough additional sales to justify the extra cost.

Testing and tracking are ongoing processes. Don't assume that last year's winning campaign will work just as well this year or next.

Test Business-to-Business Direct Mail

Robert W. Bly believes that testing various strategies and approaches, and tracking the results, are the only ways to know what works best. The four most important things to test in business-to-business direct mail include:

- Lists
- Offer, including price and discount structure
- Package format
- Sales appeal

Select a Service Bureau

There may be times when you'll need to contract with an outside company to do your telemarketing. To select the "service bureau" that's right for you, follow these criteria, adapted from Ernan Roman's book, *Integrated Direct Marketing*.

- Agency name, address, and telephone number
- Name and title of the agency contact
- Corporate affiliations
- Length of time in the business
- Current clients
- Are the service bureau's current clients your own competitors?
- Past clients
- Current/previous experience with your company
- Previous experience with similar product/service
- Previous experience with IDM campaigns
- Member of the Direct Marketing Association
- References, including three current and three past clients
- Rep training and turnover
- Rep compensation, hourly or commission
- Number of reps in the center
- Ratio of supervisors to reps
- Organizational structure
- Capacity, hours per month
- Scripting, structured scripting versus call guides

- Automation (Scripting? MIS? Telecommunications?)
- MIS (Manual or automated? How detailed?)
- Security of clients' names and other data
- Creative thinking
- Verification procedures
- Lead time to program start-up
- On-site monitoring

Add a Premium

Add a "plus" to your program by using premiums. When you send a premium through the mail, you capture the prospect's attention. You also provide the rep with a reason to call. "Has your calendar premium arrived yet?"

Keep Up with Trends

Anticipate what the next telemarketing trend will be; then go out and test it. Study your business. What are you doing right? What can you do better? Evaluate your campaigns. What have you learned from them? Have you applied this learning to future campaigns? Study other industries to see what ideas you can borrow for your own firm. Read current industry journals, trade magazines, and new business books. Listen to the latest audiotapes about management.

Develop Ongoing Customer Relationships

Roman recommends prospecting for buyers who have the potential for continued purchases, and developing and expanding the purchase activity of existing and past customers. To do this, you must have a reliable profile of the characteristics which define your potential customer base. Market research and data-base marketing can help you to create this profile.

General Advertising

Reps should track responses by their sources (direct mail, catalogs, etc.). They should also keep records of responses coming from prospects who've seen your general advertising. All general advertising should contain your toll-free 800 number. Closely track general advertising response to pinpoint a new market to test with targeted direct-response advertising. General advertising can enhance the response rates of other media.

Telemarketing's Special Role

Telemarketing plays a special role in IDM because it's a two-way communication path, which provides advantages to both the marketer and to the customer. The marketer can ask prospects questions that will enhance the value of the data base for future promotions. The prospect can seek further clarification on the offer, or ask questions regarding his specific needs.

During inbound calls, compile a basic profile on any new customers. If an established customer calls, update your data base. Probe for information on related areas of interest that may be helpful for subsequent promotions. Ask questions about additional areas of purchase interest.

During outbound calls, reps can ask a series of questions regarding needs and interests. However, the questioning shouldn't become a survey. A rep can also determine what it is about the offer that makes the prospect reluctant to purchase. Further clarification by the rep can clinch the sale. The call can also reveal the names of other possible prospects.

Benefits from Data–Base Marketing

A well-maintained data base can produce and measure true profitability, control inventory levels, track physical distribution requirements and costs, product development outlay, and corporate overhead.

Follow–Up Research

Careful tracking will provide you with statistical data about what's happening as the result of your promotion, but the question of "why" still remains. Reps can provide some qualitative information to help answer this question. Some type of follow-up research (after the campaign) can help determine how to revamp promotions to improve end results.

Telephone surveys can be administered to a sample of people who were sent the promotion, or exposed to it through magazine ads or television, or who received a telemarketing call. You could ask: "Did you read the promotion?" "What made you respond to the promotion?" Then you can determine if the promotion reached the target audience.

Create a Business–Customer Profile

Gather the following data.
- Key decision-makers in the company
- Number of employees, locations
- Product/service line
- Financial status
- Marketplace (Who are their customers?)
- Competition
- Immediate concerns
- Goals/objectives/expansion plans/trends
- Current marketing efforts (advertising, sales, distribution)

Maintaining a customer profile is an ongoing process. Every time you talk to your client, you can obtain new information. Keep the data as current and accurate as possible. Never consider the profile a static, finished document. Analyze the data to help you increase the effectiveness of your sales efforts.

Appendix

BUSINESS CONTACT PLANNER - NEW PROSPECT

1. Account Name_____

2. Address:_____

   _____ Phone:_____

3. Contact_____ Extension:_____

   Title:_____

4. Account History/Lead Info:_____

   _____

5. Goals/Purpose of Call:_____

6. Basis for Rapport:_____

7. Create Interest/Get Attention:_____

8. Questions to Ask Contact:_____

   _____

9.   Product/Service Features   Customer Benefits

   _____   _____

   _____   _____

10. Sales Message:_____

   _____

11. _____Possible Objections_____   _____Answers to Objections_____

   _____   _____

   _____   _____

   _____   _____

   Secondary offer:_____

   _____

12. Close and wrap up agreements:_____

   _____

INBOUND CAMPAIGN _____
MONTH _____

Date (Month, Day)						
Calls Offered*						
Calls Handled						
Calls Abandoned						
Calls Handled Breakdown						
- Check Call						
- Wrong Number						
- Information						
- Handled/Not Entered						
Total Contacts**						
Total Calls Handled						
Sales Breakdown***						
-						
-						
-						
Total Sales						
Abandoned						
Accessibility						

*Includes calls handled and calls abandoned.
**All callers that are given the sales presentation and have the opportunity to buy.
***List types of products/services

OUTBOUND CAMPAIGN _____

DAILY RESULTS

Date _____

RECORDS COMPLETED _____

RECORDS REMAINING _____

SALES _____

CONVERSION _____

SALES PER HOUR _____

CONTACT RATE _____

CONTACTS PER HOUR _____

ATTEMPTS PER HOUR _____

PRODUCTION HOURS _____

TOTAL CONTACTS _____

HAS PLAN _____

COMPLETIONS PER HOUR _____

Bibliography

AT&T, "AT&T Easy to Do Business With Reference Guide," 1990.

_____. "AT&T How to Use Telemarketing for Customer Service," 1983.

_____. "Making Advertising Pay Off," *Telecommunications Ideas to Grow On*, 1989.

_____. AT&T Take the Advantage! A Professional Skills Course for Telemarketing Specialists, *Group Instruction Administrator's Guide*, 1985.

_____. AT&T Telemarketing, Advertising and Promotion, 1983.

_____. "AT&T Winning Friends and Keeping Customers," Customer Service BP 1308-01, 1988.

AT&T Information Research Center, *Starting Up and Upgrading the Inhouse Telemarketing Center*, AT&T Telemarketing Update Research Program, August 1988.

Band, William A., "Creating a Customer Focused Organization," *Sales & Marketing in Canada*, August 1988.

Bayan, Richard, *Words That Sell* (Caddylak Systems, Inc., 1984).

Bencin, Richard L., "Conducting an Operations Review," *Teleprofessional Magazine*, May–June 1990.

_____. "Integrated Telemarketing with Other Direct Marketing Disciplines and Field Sales," *Journal of the American Telemarketing Association*, vol. 6, #2, February 1990.

_____. "Planning and Controlling a Strategic Telemarketing Program," *Teleprofessional Magazine*, vol. 2, #1, Spring 1989.

Bencin, Richard L., and Donald J. Jonovic, *Encyclopedia of Telemarketing* (Englewood Cliffs, NJ: Prentice-Hall, 1989).

Bly, Robert W., "The Six Most Deadly Causes of Direct Mail Disaster," *Direct Marketing Magazine*, July 1989.

Burns, Michael R., *Telemarketing: Setting Up for Success* (Norwalk, CT: Technology Marketing, 1987).

"Call Center Manager of the Month," *Service Level Newsletter*, May 1990.

Davidow, William H., and Bro Uttal, *Total Customer Service: The Ultimate Weapon* (New York: Harper & Row Publishers, 1989).

Ditkoff, Mitchell Lewis, and Steven R. McHugh, *The Idea Development Book* (New York: Idea Champions, 1989).

"800 Numbers for Customer Service: A 1988 Profile," *Society of Consumer Affairs Professionals in Business (SOCAP) & Technical Assistance Research Programs (TARP) Study*, October 1988.

Excellence Achieved, Customer Service Blueprints for Action from 50 Leading Companies (Englewood Cliffs, NJ: Prentice-Hall, 1990).

Feig, Barry, "How to Run a Focus Group," *American Demographics*, December 1989.

The Forum Corp., "How Do Companies Become Customer Focused?" *Fortune*, © 1989 Time Inc., June 5, 1989.

GE (General Electric Corp.), "Across the Board," GE Publication, September 1989.

Goldman, Alfred E., and Susan Schwartz McDonald, *The Group Depth Interview: Principles and Practices* (Englewood Cliffs, NJ: Prentice-Hall, 1987).

Goodman, John, "Improving Service Doesn't Always Require Big Investments," *The Service Edge*, vol. 3, #7, July–August 1990.

Goodman, John A., and Cynthia J. Grimm, "A Quantified Case for Improving Quality Now," *The Journal for Quality and Participation*, March 1990.

———. "Generating Measurable Profits and Incremental Sales—via an Aggressive Teleserving Department," *Journal of the American Telemarketing Association*, March 1990.

Haker, Paul, "Avoiding Seven Deadly Sins of Database Marketing," *Direct*, January 10, 1991.

Hernandez, Robert, "Delivering Customer Service Excellence," *Journal of the American Telemarketing Association*, vol. 5, #6, June 1989.

"How Can You Help Your Customer?" *The Shaw Macleod Telemarketing Report*. vol. 3, #3, Summer 1990.

Imai, Masaak, *Kaizen* (New York: McGraw-Hill, 1986).

Ingram, Mary Beth, "Angry Customers May Explode Because of Your Verbal Cues," *The Service Edge (Front Line Service)*, Lakewood Publications, vol. 3, #3, March 1990.

Isaac, Steven R., *Words for Telemarketing* (New York: Asher-Gallant Press, 1988).

Ives, Cameron, "The Basics of Renting a List That Pulls," *Inbound/Outbound Magazine*, May 1990.

Kobs, Jim, *Profitable Direct Marketing* (Lincolnwood, IL: NTC Business Books, 1979).

Koppel, Darlene Maciuba, "How to Get More from Your Monitoring," *Telemarketing Magazine*, February 1989.

———. "Make Your Script Sell," *Target Marketing Magazine*, September 1988.

———. "Motivation Boosters," DMA Telephone Marketing Council Newsletter, vol. 5, #1, Spring 1988.

———. "Seventeen Ways to Create a High-Energy Environment," *Telemarketing Magazine*, August 1989.

Kozlowski, Therese, "The Trick to Customer Service Is to Remember the Simple Steps," *The Service Edge (Front-Line Service)*, Lakewood Publications, vol. 3, #3, March 1990.

Lash, Linda, M., *The Complete Guide to Customer Service* (New York: John Wiley & Sons, 1989).

Linchitz, Joel, *The Complete Guide to Telemarketing Management* (New York: AMACOM, 1990).

Lindberg, Richard C., "Techniques for Successful Scriptwriting," *Telemarketing Magazine*, June 1990.

McHatton, Robert J., *Total Telemarketing* (New York: John Wiley & Sons, 1988).

Marx, Michael J., and Eric Adams, "A Workshop Outline to Train Managers to Hire Winners," *Telemarketing Magazine,* May 1988.

"Maximizing Customer Loyalty: The TARP Satisfaction Tracking Systems," Technical Assistance Research Programs (TARP) literature.

Memminger, Victoria, "Secrets of Success," *AT&T Focus,* vol. 4, #9, October 1990.

Parker, Glenn M., *Team Players and Teamwork* (San Francisco: Jossey-Bass Publishers, 1990).

"Peer-Based Incentive Program for CSRs at McDonnell Douglas Has High Acceptance," *Customer Service Newsletter,* vol. 16, #10, October 1988.

Penzer, Erika, "Is the Customer Always Right?", *Incentive Magazine,* May 1990.

Peoples, David A., *Presentations Plus* (New York: John Wiley & Sons, 1989).

Peters, Tom, *Thriving on Chaos* (New York: Alfred A. Knopf, 1988).

Pike, Robert W., *Creative Training Techniques Handbook* (Minneapolis: Lakewood Publications, 1989).

Roman, Ernan, *Integrated Direct Marketing* (New York: McGraw-Hill, 1988).

Rossell, Christine A., "Encouraging Complaints," *Target Marketing,* May 1987.

Sellers, Patricia, "How to Handle Customer Gripes," *Fortune,* © 1988 Time Inc., October 24, 1988.

Scholtes, Peter R., *The Team Handbook* (Madison, WI: Joiner Associates, 1989).

Thackray, John, "GE's Service Ace," *Across the Board,* September 1989.

Tice, Louis, *Investment in Excellence: An Application Guide* (Seattle: The Pacific Institute, 1983).

Townsend, Patrick L., *Commit to Quality* (New York: John Wiley & Sons, 1990).

U.S. Office of Consumer Affairs, "Increasing Customer Satisfaction (Through Effective Corporate Complaint Handling)," 1985.

Vincent, Richard, "Telemarketing and the Strategic Plan," *Journal of the American Telemarketing Association,* February 1990.

Yankeelov, Dawn Marie, "GE Answer Center Enhances Corporate Image," *Business First,* vol. 1, #13, November 1984.

Zeithaml, Valarie A., A. Parasuraman, and Leonard L. Berry, *Delivering Quality Service* (New York: The Free Press, 1990).

Zemke, Ron, and Chip R. Bell, "Ten Steps for Measuring Customer Perception of Your Service," *Service Wisdom* (Minneapolis: Lakewood Publications, 1990).

Index